Lewis and Clark

SAMUEL WILLARD CROMPTON

GREAT EXPLORERS

Jacques Cartier

James Cook

Hernan Cortes

Sir Francis Drake

Vasco da Gama

Sir Edmund Hillary

Robert de La Salle

Lewis and Clark

Ferdinand Magellan

Sir Ernest Shackleton

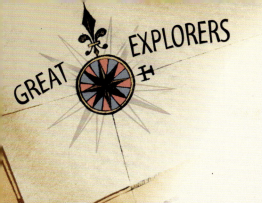

GREAT EXPLORERS

Lewis and Clark

SAMUEL WILLARD CROMPTON

CHELSEA HOUSE
PUBLISHERS

An imprint of Infobase Publishing

GREAT EXPLORERS: LEWIS AND CLARK

Copyright © 2009 by Infobase Publishing

Chelsea House
An imprint of Infobase Publishing
132 West 31st Street
New York, NY 10001

Library of Congress Cataloging-in-Publication Data
Crompton, Samuel Willard. Crompton,
  Lewis and Clark / Samuel Willard Crompton.
    p. cm. — (Great explorers)
  Includes bibliographical references and index.
  ISBN 978-1-60413-418-6 (hardcover)
  1. Lewis and Clark Expedition (1804-1806)—Juvenile literature. 2. West (U.S.)—Discovery and exploration—Juvenile literature. 3. West (U.S.)—Description and travel—Juvenile literature. 4. Lewis, Meriwether, 1774-1809—Juvenile literature. 5. Clark, William, 1770-1838—Juvenile literature. 6. Explorers—West (U.S.)—Biography—Juvenile literature. I. Title. II. Series.

  F592.7.C76 2009
  917.804'2—dc22   2009008687

Chelsea House books are available at special discounts when purchased in bulk quantities for businesses, associations, institutions, or sales promotions. Please call our Special Sales Department in New York at (212) 967-8800 or (800) 322-8755.

You can find Chelsea House on the World Wide Web at
http://www.chelseahouse.com

Series design by Lina Farinella
Cover design by Keith Trego

Printed in the United States of America

Bang FOF 10 9 8 7 6 5 4 3 2 1

This book is printed on acid-free paper.

All links and Web addresses were checked and verified to be correct at the time of publication. Because of the dynamic nature of the Web, some addresses and links may have changed since publication and may no longer be valid.

CONTENTS

He Who Never Walks

It was hot in the Rocky Mountains that August, but Captain Lewis knew the weather could change at any time.

One of two cocaptains of the Corps of Discovery, Meriwether Lewis now was the advance man, as well. He was seeking the best route for the expedition. Commissioned by President Thomas Jefferson and carrying the full credit of the United States, Captain Lewis had a great deal of responsibility. His party, which included a woman and her infant son as well as more than 30 men, had come safely thus far. The group had to obtain horses soon, however, if they were to make it over the Rocky Mountains.

The Great Divide

On August 11, 1805, Captain Lewis spotted a mounted American Indian in the distance. He could not be certain, but he suspected that this man was of the Shoshone tribe, the people that the Lewis and Clark expedition wished to contact.

Sent to explore the unknown regions of the West, Meriwether Lewis and William Clark formed a team called the Corps of Discovery and set off on one of the greatest expeditions in U.S. history. Paddling up the Missouri River, Lewis and Clark reached the Rocky Mountains and the Continental Divide. The natural boundary where rivers and streams flowing toward the Pacific Ocean are separated from those that are moving eastward.

Moving slowly forward, Lewis made signals in the sign language of the American Indians of the Great Plains. The mounted warrior let him come within about 100 yards but then turned and fled when he noticed two other white men—Lewis's fellows in the advance party—coming toward him.

Cursing his ill fortune, Lewis nonetheless took hope from the almost-meeting. If one Shoshone was here, others were, too. It was a matter of finding them.

On the next day, August 12, Lewis fulfilled a long-held desire. From the time he had been chosen to co-lead this expedition, he had been aware that the Continental Divide held the key to many of the mysteries of the far West. Every continent or major body of land has a divide, a high point from which rivers, streams, and creeks flow in opposite directions toward the two coasts. Lewis, Captain William Clark, and the rest of the Corps of Discovery had been traveling "uphill" for 16 months. They had battled their way upstream, against the current, first on the Missouri River and then on its tributaries, the entire time.

Lewis could not know that the area he was in would later be called Lemhi Pass, or that the Continental Divide eventually would form the border between the states of Montana and Idaho. All he knew was that now, for the first time since his party had left St. Louis, Missouri, in May 1804, a stream was running in a different direction. It was running to the west.

Here is how Lewis described his joy in the book *The Journals of Lewis and Clark*, as abridged by Anthony Brandt:

The road took us to the most distant fountain of the waters of the Mighty Missouri in search of which we have spent so many toilsome days and restless nights. Thus far I had accomplished one of those great objects on which my mind has been unalterably fixed for many years. Judge then of the pleasure I felt in allaying my thirst with this pure and ice-cold water.

Minutes later, as the journal notes, another member of the advance party, Hugh McNeal, stood "with a foot on each side of this little rivulet and thanked his god that he had lived to bestride the mighty & heretofore deemed endless Missouri."

The Great Reunion

On August 13, Lewis came upon three American Indian women near a stream. The women tried to run away, but he caught up with them. He put on his very best behavior and endlessly repeated *ta-Tabone*, which he believed to be the Shoshone word for "friend." Suddenly, a party of mounted warriors rode up and surrounded Lewis.

Many men would have been overcome by fright. Lewis, however, put down his rifle and walked slowly toward the mounted men, making every sign he knew of friendship and peace. He must have been quite convincing. A few hours later, he was smoking a pipe of peace with a Shoshone chief, a man named Cameahwait, in the chief's lodge.

The men's conversation was friendly but limited. Lewis knew no Shoshone, and the Shoshone knew no English. All of their communication had to be done through sign language and other gestures. Somehow, Lewis managed to convey that he and his two companions in the advance party were only a small part of a much larger group, and that it was in the Shoshones' interest to befriend them. Lewis indicated that he wished to purchase horses for his expedition. That sort of negotiation required a real interpreter, however, and Lewis's interpreter was with his main party.

Four days passed, during which Lewis sometimes was anxious and afraid. He did his best to conceal his fear that Captain Clark and the others would miss the trail he had marked. If the rest of the Corps of Discovery did not arrive, the Shoshone might well turn on Lewis. Part of their friendship with Lewis was based on the fact that he had told them he had a woman of their nation in his party. If that woman did not show up, things might go very wrong. On the evening of August 16, Lewis confided his fears to his journal:

I had mentioned to the chief several times that we had with us a woman of his nation who had been taken prisoner by the Minnetares [Blackfeet], and that by means of her I hoped to explain myself more fully than I could do with signs. Some of the party had also told the Indians that we had a man with us who was black and had short curling hair [this man was York, the slave of Captain Clark]. This had excited their curiosity very much.

Lewis's luck held. On the morning of August 17, Captain Clark and the Corps of Discovery came into view.

Clark was in the lead, but he soon was overtaken by Toussaint Charbonneau, a French Canadian, and his Shoshone wife, Sacagawea, whose name meant "Bird Woman." Hearing that her people were ahead, Sacagawea had walked forward. When she turned back to signal to Clark, she stuck her fingers into her mouth to indicate that these were, indeed, members of her tribe. Her gesture indicated that they had been suckled together.

Minutes later, Sacagawea was recognized and embraced by a tearful Shoshone woman named Jumping Fish. The two women had been childhood playmates, and both had been captured by the Blackfeet, five years before. Unlike Sacagawea, Jumping Fish had managed to escape.

Meanwhile, Lewis and Clark had a short reunion of their own. Lewis told Clark about the pass through the mountains and the Continental Divide. The men did not have long to talk, however, because Chief Cameahwait wished to speak with both of them.

Lewis and Clark entered the great tent in which Cameahwait sat on a white buffalo robe, as if he were a king or an em-

Sacagawea, the only woman in the Corps of Discovery, became an invaluable asset to the Lewis and Clark expedition. Her experience and knowledge provided the team with food and quick, levelheaded thinking in situations with potential for disaster. For Sacagawea, the journey west became meaningful for her when she realized that the Shoshone chief negotiating with Lewis and Clark was her long-lost brother, Cameahwait. *Above*, Sacagawea, Lewis, and Clark meet with a group of Shoshone.

peror. At first, the two captains did their best to communicate with the chief using sign language, but they soon grew weary of this method. They called for Sacagawea. Lewis and Clark watched her as she entered the tent, took a seat, and started to interpret. After only a moment, she leaped to her feet, started to weep, and threw her blanket over the chief.

She realized the chief was her brother.

Chief Cameahwait was moved as well. As a chief, however, he could not yield to tears or excessive emotion. Sacagawea was asked to continue interpreting. She tried, but every so often, she broke into tears once more. This was the greatest reunion of her life. She had been taken prisoner by the Blackfeet and carried a thousand miles away to live as a slave. Now, at last, she was among her own people again.

Lewis and Clark were delighted beyond measure. They had taken a chance in agreeing to bring this young woman along on the expedition. They had hoped that she might lead them to the Shoshone, but they had had no idea that she was related to the Shoshone chief. The stars were shining brightly for the Corps of Discovery.

It was still hot in the Rocky Mountains; the August weather continued as it had been on the Great Plains. If the captains had asked, however, they might have learned from the Shoshone that Rocky Mountains weather could change in an instant. The Corps of Discovery had done well to get into the mountains. Now, however, it had to get over and *through* them.

Five Flags

WHEN LEWIS AND CLARK WERE IN THE ROCKY MOUNTAINS in August 1805, they were seeking to assert American sovereignty over the land. Just a few years earlier, however, no fewer than five nations had been laying some sort of claim to the same territory.

France

In many ways, France had the best claim to the American West. The French claim was based on the explorations of René-Robert Cavelier de La Salle. In 1682, he had canoed all the way down the Mississippi River. Standing at East Pass, one of the end points of the great river, La Salle had claimed all the waters that flowed into the Mississippi for King Louis XIV of France. This is how Louisiana gained its name.

France settled the southernmost part of the vast tract that made up Louisiana but never persuaded many of its people to emigrate there. As of 1762, the year in which France turned much of the Louisiana Territory over to Spain, only about 20,000 French colonists lived in the territory.

Spain

In 1762, as France found itself on the losing side in the Seven Years' War (1754–1763) it transferred control of much of Louisiana to Spain. The kings of France and Spain were distant cousins, and it seemed better for a family member to acquire the land through a gift than for a foreign enemy to take it by force. The Spanish king gratefully accepted Louisiana, but he and his successors did not do very much with it. Spain was no longer the great power that it had been in previous centuries. The Spanish king had no spare men and little available money to expand his colonies in North America. Spain did keep a tight control on the lower Mississippi River, however, and traces of Spanish cultural heritage can still be seen in the city of New Orleans today.

Great Britain

In the eighteenth century, Great Britain was strong. Despite losing its 13 North American colonies in the American Revolutionary War (1775–1783), Great Britain maintained its commercial and naval strength. Great Britain did not have any strong claim to Louisiana because British explorers had come late to that region. Great Britain now owned Canada, however, having gained that territory from France after the Seven Years' War. It was from eastern Canada that Great Britain launched one of the greatest tours of exploration of the era.

Alexander Mackenzie, a Scot, led a British expedition that crossed Canada from the Atlantic to the Pacific. On an autumn day in 1793, Mackenzie marked a rock on Canada's western shore with the statement that he had come that far "by land," thereby establishing a British, or British-Canadian, claim to the western ocean. Even Great Britain, with all its military and commercial strength, had a rival in the far West, however.

Russia

Russia had long been regarded with suspicion by her European neighbors. Was Russia really a European country, or was it an Asian one? Because of the extent of Russia's territory, the question could not be answered definitively, even by geographers. Russia surprised Great Britain, France, Spain, and almost everyone else, however, when it launched an exploration of North America from the west. The first Russian explorers ventured to Alaska in the 1740s. By 1800, Russia was looking with interest at what are now the states of Washington, Oregon, and California.

The United States

The fifth nation competing to plant its flag in the region was, of course, the United States. By the time Lewis and Clark reached the Continental Divide, there were 17 states in the Union.

Today, when one looks at a map, it may appear obvious that the United States eventually would extend from sea to shining sea. As late as 1800, however, there still was some doubt about the young nation's ability to expand all the way westward. The United States was firmly planted on the eastern seaboard and, in theory, had better access to the Far West than any other nation. An American trek overland to the West Coast, however, probably would take longer than a voyage from Great Britain to the Oregon Territory. This was true even though an English ship would have to travel around the bottom of South America to reach the Pacific Northwest. As for the Russians, they seemed well positioned in Alaska to expand their territory down the length of North America's western coast.

What the United States had in its favor was the energetic capacity of those men and women among its citizens who were accustomed to frontier life. Already, many families that had grown up along the East Coast had crossed the Appalachian Mountains in search of new lands in which to settle. Pioneers like these were

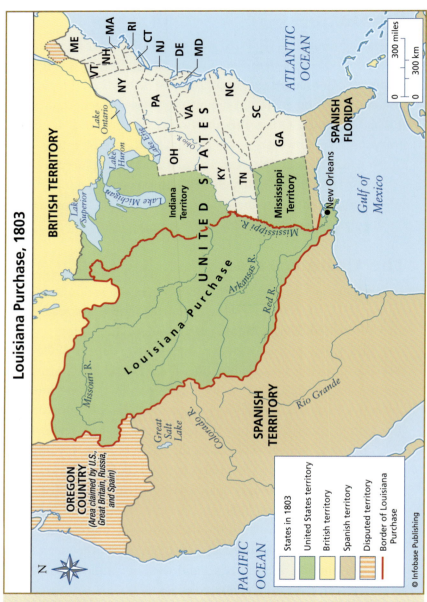

Louisiana Purchase, 1803

BRITISH TERRITORY

UNITED STATES

Louisiana Purchase

SPANISH TERRITORY

OREGON COUNTRY
(Area claimed by U.S., Great Britain, Russia, and Spain)

SPANISH FLORIDA

ME
NH
VT
MA
RI
CT
NY
NJ
DE
MD
PA
OH
VA
KY
TN
NC
SC
GA

Indiana Territory

Mississippi Territory

New Orleans

ATLANTIC OCEAN

Gulf of Mexico

PACIFIC OCEAN

Lake Superior
Lake Michigan
Lake Huron
Lake Ontario
Lake Erie

Ohio R.
Mississippi R.
Missouri R.
Arkansas R.
Red R.
Great Salt Lake
Colorado R.
Rio Grande

N

0   300 miles
0   300 km

States in 1803
United States territory
British territory
Spanish territory
Disputed territory
Border of Louisiana Purchase

© Infobase Publishing

Determined to control the French port of New Orleans, President Thomas Jefferson sent envoys to negotiate a land sale with Napoleon Bonaparte, who was hoping to establish a presence in North America. Without any other French colonies nearby, Napoleon began to turn his attention back toward conquering Europe and agreed to sell the entire Louisiana Territory. Almost overnight, the United States doubled in size.

well suited to continue their journeys of discovery into the Far West. There were other people to consider, however.

American Indians

Today, we do not say that there were six flags competing for the North American continent because there was no single American Indian nation. Instead, there were hundreds of different American Indian tribes. Some of these peoples considered their tribal neighbors to be great dangers, sometimes even greater dangers than the invading white men. Had the American Indian tribes west of the Mississippi River joined forces, they might have been able to resist the European and American explorers. That type of tribal unity did not exist, however.

Shifting Sands

At the end of the eighteenth century and the beginning of the nineteenth, a number of political and diplomatic changes took place that had an impact on the exploration and settlement of the American far West.

In 1799, a general named Napoleon Bonaparte, born in Corsica but educated in France, seized power in France. He declared a new government, with himself at its head as first consul.

In 1800, Thomas Jefferson was elected the third president of the United States. The election was so close that it had to be decided in the U.S. House of Representatives, according to the Constitution. This happens when neither candidate wins a majority in the Electoral College.

Late in 1800, while the American presidential election was still in doubt, Napoleon forced the king of Spain to return the Louisiana Territory to France. All of the land between the Mississippi River and the Rocky Mountains now returned to French control.

President Jefferson took the oath of office in March 1801. His critics had claimed that Jefferson was biased in favor of the French and was too ready to accommodate them in foreign policy. Nonetheless, as described in Dumas Malone's *Jefferson and His Time*, when Jefferson learned of Napoleon's diplomatic move, he wrote this, in a letter to a friend: "The day France takes possession of New Orleans . . . is the day we must marry ourselves to the British fleet and nation." Jefferson would not allow a new French empire to be established in America, even if that meant joining forces with the British.

CAUGHT BETWEEN TWO EMPIRES

During the first 25 years of its existence, the young United States was caught between the power of the existing British Empire and the new French Empire created by Napoleon Bonaparte.

The French Revolution erupted in 1789, the same year in which George Washington became the first president of the United States. In 1793, the French executed their king, Louis XIV, and the country declared itself a republic. In that same year, Great Britain, Spain, Austria, and Prussia all went to war against France.

In the decade that followed, France made every effort to involve the United States in its struggle against Great Britain. Reminding the Americans that the French had helped the United States during the American Revolution, the new French leaders practically demanded that the United States declare war against England. President George Washington wisely refused to do so, however; he issued a formal declaration of neutrality in 1793.

The remaining years of Washington's term in office were partially spoiled by conflicts within his administration. Thomas Jefferson, the secretary of state, showed a preference for the French; Alexander Hamilton, the secretary of the treasury, showed a preference for the British. Things grew even worse when both Great Britain and France began to force American sailors to serve on British and French ships.

Napoleon's Gambit

Napoleon desired a new American empire. In 1801 and 1802, he sent thousands of his best troops, led by his brother-in-law General Charles Leclerc, to Haiti, to put down a slave rebellion. Haiti was important to the French for its sugar plantations, but France also saw control of this Caribbean outpost as a first step toward establishing a French military presence in Louisiana. If the French could pacify Haiti, they could use its ports as bases for communications with and the shipment of supplies to Louisiana.

This practice was called *impressment*. It meant that British and French ships stopped American ships and "pressed" American sailors into service aboard the Europeans' vessels. Both Great Britain and France violated American neutrality in the process. Great Britain, with its larger navy and merchant marine, was the bigger offender, however. President Washington managed to keep the United States at peace, but the issue of impressment bedeviled both his last years in office and the four years of the John Adams administration that followed.

When Thomas Jefferson came to office in 1801, he was in a better position than either of his predecessors to deal with Great Britain and France. Great Britain and France were at peace, if only for a short while. Furthermore, Jefferson was able to take advantage of the aftermath of France's failed invasion of Haiti in 1801 and 1802 to obtain the vast territory that the United States gained from France in 1803 in the Louisiana Purchase. The matter of impressment resurfaced in 1804 and 1805, however, and it became the thorniest problem of Jefferson's second term in office.

Impressment finally ended in 1814, during the administration of President James Madison, with the signing of the Treaty of Ghent. That treaty ended the War of 1812 between the United States and Great Britain. By that time, thanks to the growth of its armed forces and to the geographic explorations of Lewis and Clark, the United States found itself in a stronger position. Americans of the period remembered impressments as one of the most dangerous issues of their time, however.

President Jefferson was alarmed by the French buildup in Haiti. Soon after he learned of the size of the French presence there, he sent two diplomats to Paris, the French capital, with an offer to purchase the city of New Orleans. James Monroe and Robert Livingston were authorized to spend up to two million dollars to buy New Orleans from France.

When Livingston and Monroe went to the French foreign minister to make their offer, they were astonished by his reply. If France was going to sell New Orleans, it might as well sell the entire Louisiana Territory. What good was that vast tract, after all, without the city that bundled and shipped its products?

The American diplomats were astounded. Only later did they learn that Napoleon's venture into Haiti had been an un-qualified disaster. Many of the French troops—and Napoleon's brother-in-law—had died of yellow fever. The Haitian slave revolt had turned into the first successful one of its kind, and France was withdrawing from the Western Hemisphere.

Livingston and Monroe could hardly believe their great luck. They negotiated and within a few weeks had agreed to and signed the treaty that ceded the Louisiana Purchase to the United States. Under the agreement, all the land between the Mississippi River and the Rocky Mountains went to the United States. The purchase price was $15 million, which worked out to about three cents per acre. (No one knew this at the time, of course, as the territory had not yet been surveyed).

Scruples of Conscience

President Jefferson received the news of the purchase in the sum-mer of 1803. His two emissaries had acquired the entire Louisiana Territory, effectively doubling the size of the United States.

Jefferson was overcome with joy, but he had to face a pain-ful fact: The purchase went against his principles. Throughout the 1790s and into his first term as president, Jefferson had been an advocate of what is called strict constructionism. To a strict constructionist, the words of the United States Constitution had to be applied strictly to each situation that might arise. Because there was no clause in the Constitution that applied to the purchase of foreign lands or to additions to the size of the United States, Jefferson had to choose between his Constitutional principles and the greatest land offer of his presidency (and perhaps of any other presidency).

He accepted. He forwarded the Purchase Treaty to the U.S. Senate with a recommendation that it be accepted as it stood. The Senate followed suit, and by the end of 1803, the United States had taken a huge step toward raising the stars and stripes in place of the other flags that had stood in the way of the nation's westward expansion.

Royal Spain? It had given its land to France.

Imperial France? It had sold its land to the United States.

Imperial Great Britain? It still was a threat in the Pacific Northwest, but it had no claim on the Great Plains.

Czarist Russia? There still was some threat from that direction.

The American Indian tribes? They would have to learn that they had a new sovereign now, one with 17 stars on its flag.

The Commission

On January 18, 1803, three months before the Louisiana Purchase Treaty was signed, President Jefferson sent a secret message to Congress:

> The river Missouri and the Indians inhabiting it are not as well known as is rendered desirable by their connection with the Mississippi, and consequently with us. It is, however, understood, that the country on that river is inhabited by numerous tribes, who furnish great supplies of furs and peltry to the trade of another nation [British Canada].

The message had to do with trade and the potential for its growth. The president asked for, and Congress granted, a special appropriation of $2,500 for an exploring tour of the lands on both sides of the Missouri River.

Before leading the exploration team into the West, Meriwether Lewis had managed his family's plantation, Locust Hill, and joined the military. His participation in suppressing the Whiskey Rebellion and his service during the Northwest Indian War earned him several promotions to the rank of captain. Lewis, whose father was neighbors with Thomas Jefferson, also worked as the president's private secretary in the White House.

Captain Lewis

President Jefferson acted before he even knew of the Louisiana Purchase. When that news arrived, he became even more enthusiastic about the need to explore in the Far West. To whom would he turn, however?

Meriwether Lewis was born in Albemarle County, Virginia, in 1774. He was a true son of the frontier. His father was a successful tobacco planter, but Lewis was orphaned at about the age of 10 and had to make his own way in life. He helped his mother to manage the family estate in the foothills of the Blue Ridge Mountains and, while still young, also traveled as far as the frontier of Georgia.

Lewis joined the United States Army in 1790 and rose to the rank of lieutenant. His superiors noted his dash and daring, but he also was moody and had an inclination to drink too much alcohol. As an ensign, young Meriwether Lewis was court-martialed for drinking, but he escaped with a light punishment.

In 1801, almost as soon as he was sworn in as president, Thomas Jefferson asked Lewis to come to Washington to serve as his private and confidential secretary. Jefferson had known Lewis's father, and Lewis had grown up almost within sight of Jefferson's Virginia estate. Moreover, Jefferson and Lewis shared a great interest in the Far West. Like many Virginians of their time, Jefferson and Lewis had been inspired by the stories of men such as Daniel Boone and John Filson. The same sort of men would be needed to explore the West.

As the president's secretary, Lewis knew about the Louisiana Purchase and the possibilities it opened for the future. Even so, he was thrilled—and more than a little surprised—when the president asked him to be the commander of what would be known as the Corps of Discovery. Lewis accepted, and the great exploratory expedition was about to get under way.

Philadelphia

Soon after he received his appointment, Captain Lewis left for Philadelphia. There, he wanted to confer with the best scientific and medical minds of the day. Since the time of Benjamin Franklin (who had died in 1790), Philadelphia had housed the nation's largest library and its greatest assemblage of doctors of

JEFFERSON'S WHITE HOUSE

White House is a modern, twentieth-century term; most presidents before 1900 called the house in which they lived the Executive Mansion. The White House was constructed on a spot that overlooks the Potomac River. To Jefferson and the men of his generation, the Potomac was a symbol of the gateway to the American West.

Jefferson came to the White House as a widower (his wife had died in 1782), and he did much of the entertaining himself. Visitors often were astonished when the president of the United States met them at the door and ushered them into a drawing room. President Jefferson had cooks in his kitchens, but he, too, liked to cook. He liked fine food, and he had a keen appreciation for wines. Meriwether Lewis was privileged to share in this life.

Lewis was constantly busy during his White House years. He drafted correspondence and brainstormed with the president on many matters. Sadly, neither Jefferson nor Lewis left a good description of their conversations. We can assume, however, that these two Virginians understood each other and enjoyed working together. When it came time to select a person to lead the great Western expedition, Jefferson chose Lewis.

Like many American presidents, Jefferson found his first term much more enjoyable than his second. The years from 1801 to 1805 were filled with success, including the Louisiana Purchase and a successful war against the Barbary pirates (Muslim pirates who attacked American ships sailing in the Mediterranean). The years from 1805 to 1809 were plagued by foreign affairs, most notably the conflict with Great Britain about the impressment of American sailors to serve in the British Navy.

On March 4, 1809—the day on which his successor, James Madison, was sworn in as president—Jefferson rode from the White House to his beloved home at Monticello, Virginia. Although he lived for 15 more years, the former president never crossed the Potomac again.

medicine. In 1803, Philadelphia definitely was the repository of the nation's knowledge.

Lewis came to Philadelphia in search of maps, medicine, guns, and just about anything else that might be needed on the expedition. The explorers would not be able to acquire anything after they passed the farthest line of western settlements. At that time, that point was near St. Louis, in the Louisiana Territory (today's St. Louis, Missouri). Lewis conferred with the best mapmakers of the day, but they confessed that their knowledge of the land and water along the expedition's projected route became vague as one started to ascend the Missouri River.

In the city, Lewis also met with Doctor Benjamin Rush, a pioneer in the fight against yellow fever. The disease had killed many Philadelphians in the summer of 1794. To deal with the fever, Doctor Rush gave Lewis some Peruvian bark, which contained quinine. He also gave him laxatives, some so powerful that people called them "Rush's thunderclappers." Neither Rush nor any other doctor of the time knew much about the transmission and spread of disease. They were experts, however, in such skills as binding up wounds and setting broken limbs. Lewis profited from the time he spent with Doctor Rush.

After his visit to Philadelphia, Lewis spent some time at the federal arsenal at Harpers Ferry, Virginia. There, he requisitioned an enormous amount of supplies for the expedition. He knew that his men would have to bring almost every implement of civilization with them. Nothing, from knives to safety pins, was available on the western side of the Mississippi River.

The Invitation

President Jefferson made Lewis the sole commander of the expedition. Lewis, however, in what turned out to be a wise move, decided that he needed a co-commander for the journey. He knew many men of quality and endurance, but the more he

William Clark, a one-time superior officer and friend of Meriwether Lewis, was asked to help lead the Corps of Discovery. Clark grew up on the frontier and was experienced in mapmaking, interacting with American Indians, and living in the wilderness.

pondered the matter, the more he came to believe that William Clark of Kentucky should be his first choice.

Born in Virginia in 1770, William Clark came from a leading family of American frontiersmen. His much older brother, Colonel George Rogers Clark, had led Kentucky and Ohio frontiersmen in two of the most hazardous and successful wilderness marches of the Revolutionary War, during which they had captured the Illinois towns of Kaskaskia and Vincennes from the British. In March 1785, Clark, his parents, his three sisters, and the family's slaves moved to a Kentucky plantation called Mulberry Hill. Here Clark was taught wilderness survival skills by his brother George. In 1789, at the age of 19, Clark started his military career with a volunteer militia fighting American Indians north of the Ohio River.

As recorded in Stephen Ambrose's *Undaunted Courage*, on June 19, 1803, Lewis wrote to Captain William Clark of Kentucky, asking him to join the Corps of Discovery:

> [I]f therefore there is anything under those circumstances, in this enterprise, which would induce you to participate with me in its fatigues, its dangers, and its honors, believe me there is no man on earth with whom I should feel equal pleasure in sharing them as with yourself.

The two men had not seen each other in years. Back in 1794, however, Ensign Meriwether Lewis had been assigned temporarily to Lieutenant William Clark's rifle company. The two were of similar spirit, although not of similar temperament. Both had Virginia in their blood, and both were thrilled of the thought of crossing the mountains. Clark already had spent half of his life on the western side of the Appalachians.

In his letter to Clark, Lewis also commented on the need to recruit men for the expedition: "Some good hunters, stout, healthy, unmarried men, accustomed to the woods, and capable of bearing bodily fatigue in a pretty considerable degree."

Meriwether Lewis's one-time commander was four years older than Lewis. When Clark received the invitation to serve as co-commander of the Corps of Discovery, he accepted.

> Dear Lewis
>
> I received by yesterday's mail your letter of the 19th: the contents of which I received with much pleasure. The

enterprise and mission is such as I have long anticipated & am much pleased with. . . . This is an immense undertaking freighted with numerous difficulties, but my friend I can assure you that no man lives with whom I would prefer to undertake and share the difficulties of such a trip than yourself.

Lewis's decision to recruit Clark as his co-commander has to rank as one of his wisest moves. Although the president had entrusted him with total command, Lewis was all too aware of what he called the "fatigues" and "dangers" of the journey. He needed a co-commander—a man on whom he could rely totally, and who could pick up the reins of leadership if necessary.

Pittsburgh

When Lewis wrote to Clark, Lewis was on the East Coast. Clark was at his family home, near the Falls of the Ohio River. Because the two men could not link up right away, it made sense for them to divide responsibilities and then unite later in the year. In the autumn of 1803, Lewis was at Pittsburgh, where the Allegheny and Monongahela rivers meet. Clark was in Kentucky. Both men were occupied with matters concerning the recruitment and acquiring of men and matériel (equipment and supplies).

Around this time, Lewis received his official instructions from President Jefferson. Although Lewis had made Clark co-leader of the expedition, the formal documents still were addressed to Lewis only. As quoted in Brandt's abridgement of the *Journals of Lewis and Clark*,

"The object of your mission is to explore the Missouri River, & such principal stream of it, as, by its course and communication with the waters of the Pacific Ocean, may offer the most direct & practicable water communication across this continent, for the purposes of commerce."

EQUIPPING THE EXPEDITION

Altogether Lewis spent $2,324 on gear. Lewis and Clark went west as well equipped as any exploring expedition.

- 55-foot (17-meter) keelboat
- 2 pirogues (open boats)
- Square sail (also called a broad sail)
- 35 oars
- 2 horses
- 150 Yards (140 meters) of cloth to be oiled and sewn into tents and sheets
- 6 large needles, 4,600 sewing needles
- Pliers, chisels, handsaws, 25 hatchets
- Oilskin bags, whetstones
- 30 steels for striking or making fire
- Iron corn mill
- 2 dozen tablespoons
- Mosquito curtains
- 10.5 pounds (5 kilograms) of fishing hooks and fishing lines
- 12 pounds (5.4 kilograms) of soap
- 193 pounds (87.5 kilograms) of "portable soup"
- 3 bushels (106 liters) of salt
- Writing paper, ink and crayons
- 45 flannel shirts
- 20 coats
- 15 frocks
- Shoes, 30 stockings
- Woolen pants, 15 pairs wool overalls
- 15 blankets
- Knapsacks
- 50 dozen Dr. Rush's patented "Rush's Thunderclapper" pills
- Lancets, forceps, syringes, tourniquets
- 1,300 doses of physic
- 1,100 doses of emetic
- 3,500 doses of diaphoretic (sweat inducer)
- Additional drugs
- 15 prototype Model 1803 muzzle-loading .54-caliber rifles, or "Kentucky Rifles"
- 15 gun slings
- 24 large knives
- Powder horns

500 rifle flints
420 pounds (191 kilograms) of sheet lead for bullets
176 pounds (80 kilograms) of gunpowder packed in 52 lead canisters
1 long-barreled rifle that fired its bullet with compressed air, rather than by flint, spark, and powder
Surveyor's compass
Hand compass
1 Hadley's quadrant
1 telescope
3 thermometers
2 sextants
1 set of plotting instruments
1 chronometer (needed to calculate longitude; at $250 it was the most expensive item)
1 portable microscope
1 tape measure
A Practical Introduction to Spherics and Nautical Astronomy
Antoine Simon's *Le Page du Pratz's History of Louisiana*
Barton's *Elements of Botany*
Dictionary (4-volume)
Linnaeus (2-volume edition), the Latin classification of plants
Richard Kirwan's *Elements of Mineralogy*
The Nautical Almanac and Astronomical Ephemeris
Tables for finding longitude and latitude
Map of the Great Bend of the Missouri River

They also bought presents for the American Indians they would meet:

12 dozen pocket mirrors
144 small scissors
10 pounds (4.5 kilograms) of sewing thread
Silk ribbons, Ivory combs, handkerchiefs
Yards of bright-colored cloth
130 rolls of tobacco
Tomahawks that doubled as pipes
288 knives
8 brass kettles
Vermilion face paint
20 pounds (9 kilograms) of assorted beads, mostly blue
5 pounds (2 kilograms) of small, white, glass beads
288 brass thimbles
Armbands
Ear trinkets

Although Jefferson has been accused of showing a bias toward agriculture and against industry, he was all in favor of commerce. Indeed, he thought that commerce would be the life-blood of the nation in the future. The president also instructed Lewis (and, by implication, Clark) to discover the most important details about the American Indian tribes that lived along their route. According to Jefferson, Lewis was to find out:

> [the] names of the nations & their numbers
> the extent & limit of their possessions;
> their relations with other tribes or nations;
> their language, traditions, monuments.

As a precaution against the Corps of Discovery's being marooned on the West Coast, President Jefferson gave Captain Lewis a bill of credit. Lewis was to draw on this for any funds necessary to return to the United States by ship. Jefferson did all that he could, short of sending a ship himself, to ensure the success of the Corps of Discovery. Now it was up to the two captains to make the best of what they had.

Lewis set out by boat from Pittsburgh on August 31, 1803. Almost from the beginning, he met with something that would prove to be an enduring thorn in the expedition's side: sandbars. The lower Ohio River was full of driftwood and sand; these sometimes joined together to create formidable obstacles to navigation. Lewis and his company of six men made slow progress during the first two weeks, as they edged their way down the Ohio River.

Clark, meanwhile, was at the Falls of the Ohio, recruiting men for the expedition. There were many volunteers, but not all of them had the right stuff. Lewis and Clark wanted hardy backwoodsmen, men who were accustomed to living away from civilization for months at a time. Some of the best of these men now were too old, however, after having spent their best years finding and blazing trails over the Appalachian Mountains.

Clark knew that he had to look for younger men. He found several of them in the ranks of the U.S. Army:

John Ordway was a sergeant in the Army when he joined the Corps of Discovery.

Patrick Gass joined as a private but soon became a sergeant.

John Colter, a Virginian, already was known as a formidable backwoodsman and fur trapper.

Pierre Cruzatte was a French Canadian; he was as handy with his violin as he was with a canoe paddle.

The men were rowdy and Lewis and Clark experienced some discipline troubles. Army men and former fur trappers alike bridled at their commanders' early attempts at discipline. On more than one occasion, in fact, Lewis and Clark had to order the administration of lashes.

Union

Lewis and his small band met Clark and his larger party at the end of October 1803. Originally, the plan had been for the combined group to set off for the Lower Missouri River. It now was too late in the season, however, and the captains agreed to spend the winter near St. Louis. They did not stay within the town, for fear that that might give the men too much freedom. Instead, the Corps of Discovery spent the winter of 1803–1804 on the east bank of the Mississippi, about seven miles from St. Louis.

Lewis remained in St. Louis for most of the winter, but Clark stayed with the men at Wood Creek, just across from the mouth of the Missouri River. Clark drilled the men while Lewis arranged things on the diplomatic front. Among other duties, Lewis negotiated with the Spanish governor of Upper Louisiana. Although Spain had transferred the area to Napoleon, and Napoleon had sold the land to the United States, the switches in government had yet to take place on the ground. Lewis tried to depict his exploring party as simply a slightly larger version of a fur-trapping expedition, but the Spanish governor was not deceived. He wrote that "he [Lewis] has the reputation of being a very well educated man and of many talents." The governor knew that President Jefferson would not send such a man on an unimportant mission.

Setting Out

The Lewis and Clark expedition officially commenced on Monday, May 14, 1804. The two captains were not together, however; Lewis was still in town. It fell to Clark to give the first order, as noted in Brandt's abridgement of the journals:

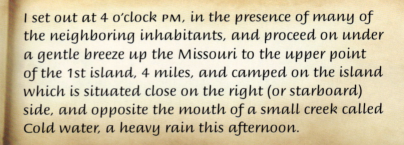

I set out at 4 o'clock PM, in the presence of many of the neighboring inhabitants, and proceed on under a gentle breeze up the Missouri to the upper point of the 1st island, 4 miles, and camped on the island which is situated close on the right (or starboard) side, and opposite the mouth of a small creek called Cold water, a heavy rain this afternoon.

The "heavy rain" was a portent of things to come.

Up the Big Muddy

WHEN IT COMES TO AMERICAN RIVERS, THE MISSISSIPPI IS THE most well-known. It is, after all, the biggest and most productive of all American rivers. It carries millions of tons of silt from the Midwest to the Gulf of Mexico. The Mississippi would be only two-thirds it current size, and would run with only about half its enormous strength, however, if the muddy Missouri did not flow into it. The Big Muddy feeds the Father of Waters.

Upstream

Captain Lewis joined the expedition a few days after it began. Fully united, the Corps of Discovery began to make its way up the Missouri River.

The expedition traveled in three vessels. They were propelled primarily by oars, but two of the boats had sails as well. The late spring weather was generally fine, but the oarsmen—very few expedition members escaped oar duty—had to put their backs into their job because the Missouri was running with a fury. The river was carrying snowmelt from the distant Rocky Mountains.

The fierce current created problems. The Missouri River was and is a tricky body of water. Along the river, great mud cliffs can form, stand for weeks or even months, and then crash suddenly into the water. The river even changes course at times and wears new channels into the soil. Within a week or two of starting out, however, the Corps of Discovery had developed a rhythm for combating the Missouri and the other elements. Clark usually remained onboard one of the boats, often holding a tiller, while Lewis, accompanied by his beloved Newfoundland dog, Seaman, often walked along the south bank of the river. Between them, Lewis and Clark caught sight of many dangers and steered the boats away from them.

Some difficulties could not be evaded, however. At times, mud cliffs along the banks gave way. At other times, the boats got stuck in shallow waters. At such times, all of the men got into the water to push the boats out of the shallows. To say, as the journals do, that this was "brisk" or "warm" work was an understatement, indeed. This excerpt from Brandt's abridgement of the journals shows Monday, June 18, as an example:

> Some hard rain last night, and some hard showers this morning which delay our work very much. Sent out six hunters in the prairie on the left shore, they kill 5 deer & caught a bear, which very large and fat. The party to work at the oars, make rope, & jerk their meat [cut into strips and dried in the sun] all day. Dry our wet sails &. In the evening. The mosquitoes very bad.

While preparing for the mission, Lewis studied under Dr. Benjamin Rush, a famous physician at the time, to gain an understanding of basic medical treatment for potential injuries or ailments in the wilderness. Along with information learned during his crash course, Lewis also took a small chest full of equipment and medicines that included laxatives and painkillers.

Any one of the tasks and animals mentioned, such as mosquitoes, might put fear into present-day travelers. As for catching a bear, one wonders how the men did it. Was the bear led to fall into a bear trap?

The First Loss

As the Corps of Discovery moved upriver, the men grew in strength. Their muscles developed as a result of the paddling. They also suffered from a variety of ailments, however. Dysentery (an inflammatory disorder of the lower intestinal tract) came first.

Captain Clark rightly guessed that the brackish water of the Missouri contributed to the dysentery, but he and Captain Lewis still had to minister to the sick men. That was only the beginning.

Men began to develop boils on their skin and bumps that Lewis and Clark called "tumers." (It is believed that these bumps had nothing to do with cancer.) Lewis himself became quite ill after breathing in some vapors around some lumps of coal. In most cases, the captains and the men recovered quickly. This was not true of Sergeant Charles Floyd. On August 19, Clark wrote that "[He] is taken very bad all at once with a biliose chorlick [a bilious colic], we attempt to relive him without success as yet, he gets worse, and we are much alarmed at his situation, all [give] attention to him."

Floyd probably had a ruptured appendix. Two weeks earlier, he had become very sick but had recovered. This time, however, he worsened, and neither Lewis nor Clark could do anything for him. He died on Monday, August 20. His last words are given as "I am going away . . . I want you to write me a letter."

The Corps of Discovery buried Floyd on a bluff, half a mile below a river to which they gave his name. In the journal, Clark indicated the strong feelings that the men had for their fallen comrade: "This man at all times gave us proofs of his firmness and determined resolution to do service to his country and honor to himself."

Not all members of the group did their service as well or as willingly as Floyd. Just days before Floyd's death, Lewis and Clark had sentenced one man to 50 lashes for desertion and another man to 100 lashes for allowing the desertion to take place.

The First Meetings

At about the time that the expedition lost Sergeant Floyd (whose rank was given to Private Gass), the Corps of Discovery started to meet large numbers of American Indians. Lewis and Clark had decided in advance how to act toward them. Now they had to put their theory into practice.

Following President Jefferson's instructions, the two captains wished both to befriend the American Indians and to convey to them that they now were under the sovereignty of the United States of America. This would be tricky in almost any situation, with any people. Given the pride of the Great Plains

Medals bearing Thomas Jefferson's likeness were carried by Lewis and Clark during their expedition to distribute to the American Indians they would encounter on the way. Though the explorers and the U.S. government saw the acceptance of these medals as recognition of their sovereignty, most American Indians interpreted the giving of these tokens as gestures of equality and peace.

tribes, however, Lewis and Clark would have to be diplomatic magicians to pull it off.

The explorers met the first American Indians, members of the Oto tribe, on August 3. Lewis and Clark set up an awning on shore, and Lewis gave a speech. This was followed by the presentation of gifts to the major chiefs of the group. The gifts included beads, mirrors, and medals showing President Jefferson's likeness. Perhaps most important, from Lewis and

Clark's point of view, were the certificates that they handed out. The text of each document started with President Jefferson's name and title, printed in boldface type. That was followed by words that expressed the desire of the United States to remain in "peace, harmony, and good neighborhood" with the American Indian tribes. In truth, however, the explorers required the reverse from their newly met American Indian neighbors. Lewis made a point of addressing the Oto as inferiors, as described in Reuben Gold Thwaites' *Journals of Lewis and Clark*: "Children, we have been sent by the great chief of the Seventeen great nations. . . . [You] must obey the commands of their great chief, the President who is now your only great father."

All went well until the Corps of Discovery met the Teton Sioux.

Great Danger

The Teton Sioux were relative newcomers to the region that today is Nebraska. They did not yet possess the vast herds of horses of which their sons and grandsons would boast. They were, however, a warlike group who demanded tolls from white traders passing through their territory that bullied their American Indian neighbors. In one of his first conversations with the Teton Sioux, Captain Lewis learned that they had attacked a neighboring tribe, killed at least 40 people, and taken twice as many prisoners.

A handful of French and Spanish traders, operating out of St. Louis, had traveled this section of the Missouri River before Lewis and Clark, but the traders either had been turned back by the Sioux or had had their trade goods confiscated for sale to other tribal groups. Lewis and Clark knew the reputation of the Teton Sioux, and especially the reputation of one of their chiefs, who went by the name of the Partisan. The expedition's first contact with the Sioux was made on September 25.

In the journal of the expedition, Captain Clark relates how several Sioux leaders, including the Partisan, came aboard their

HORSES AND BUFFALO

Vast herds of buffalo had roamed the Great Plains for untold centuries. Horses, however, were relative newcomers to the region.

Ever since the sixteenth century, the time of the Spanish conquistador Francisco Vásquez de Coronado, Europeans had been vaguely aware that a different kind of animal lived in the American West. It was a creature of immense strength and speed whose furry hide provided wonderful warmth. Few, if any, Europeans knew of these animals vast numbers, however.

Lewis and Clark were among the first explorers of the American West to appreciate how many buffalo there were. On one occasion, Lewis, who was a careful observer, estimated that he could see 3,500 buffalo on one vast section of open plain. There is no way to say for certain how many buffalo existed in all, but later estimates run to as many as 50 million.

Buffalo meat was prized by the American Indians, and buffalo fur had no equal as a source of warmth. Until the horse made its appearance, however, the American Indians could catch or kill only a few buffalo at a time.

The first horses came to the Great Plains from Spanish Mexico. Exactly when they arrived on the Plains remains a mystery, however. Any American Indian tribe that had horses before its rivals had an enormous advantage, and quite a few wars erupted among the Plains tribes during the eighteenth century. It is generally accepted that by about 1800, most of the American Indian tribes on the Great Plains had horses. The horses changed their lives.

Horses gave the Plains Indians great mobility. Tribes that had remained within a 100-mile radius suddenly expanded their territories to 500 miles or more. Hunting buffalo became much easier—although not necessarily safer—with the horse. It is difficult to think of any way in which the appearance of the horse did not improve the lives of the Great Plains tribes. Certainly, the peoples of the Plains knew what a prize they had found. They lavished care and attention on these creatures that transformed their lives.

boats. The captains offered brandy to these chiefs. The Sioux drank and then responded with hostility. Clark took charge of one of the smaller boats of the expedition and paddled it to the west side of the river. There, he hoped to be rid of the chiefs. One of the chiefs seized the boat's rope, or line, as soon as the boat came ashore, however, and other members of the Sioux party threatened Clark. The Sioux insisted that he could not leave until he and his men distributed more gifts. Thwaites' *Journals of Lewis and Clark* quotes Clark: "His gestures were of such a personal nature that I felt myself compelled to draw my sword (and made a signal to the boat to prepare for action), at this motion Captain Lewis ordered all under arms in the boat. . . . I felt myself warm & spoke in very positive terms."

By now, most of the Teton Sioux warriors on the west bank had their bows strung and their arrows out of their quivers, although not yet positioned to fire. Captain Lewis, meanwhile, had manned one of the swivel guns aboard the large boat, and every member of the Corps of Discovery was ready for a fight.

The bravery of the explorers cannot be disputed; every indication was that they would perish. There were hundreds of Sioux warriors in the vicinity, and all of them knew the terrain and the river's waters better than any member of the Corps of Discovery.

The determination of the men of the expedition to stand and fight won the day. The Teton Sioux were used to dealing with small parties of French and Spanish traders who were more eager to make money than to make a point. For several years, the Sioux had been the bullies of this stretch of the Missouri River. The Sioux did not want to make this an all-out fight, however. The fact that they surely would win was less important than the fact that they would suffer many casualties. They were not prepared for that. The confrontation on the riverbank turned into a standoff. By standing firm, the Americans won a moral victory.

Lewis and Clark spent another two days in the neighborhood of the Teton Sioux. During that time, the explorers constantly were on watch. They did not feel safe again until they had put this section of the river behind them. They had won, however, and against heavy odds. The Corps of Discovery had not come to grief.

The Coming of Winter

Although October can be a pleasant month on the Great Plains, Lewis and Clark soon began to think about setting up winter quarters. Not long after leaving the Teton Sioux (a sorrowful parting for neither party), they did so.

As the Corps of Discovery continued up the Missouri, it entered the territory of the Mandan Indians, a group known to French explorers since the 1730s. The Mandan had been a large tribe when French fur trappers first encountered them, but endless wars with the Sioux and a devastating smallpox epidemic had reduced their numbers. The Mandan lived in better comfort than most American Indians, however, and the spaciousness of their lodges was known to anyone who came their way. That way led through what is now North Dakota.

Lewis, Clark, and their company came upon the first Mandan groups toward the end of October. The explorers met with the leading tribal chiefs and asked permission to build a lodge of their own for the winter. This request was a little contradictory in view of the fact that at the same time, Lewis and Clark asserted the sovereignty of President Jefferson and the United States over Mandan lands. No offense was taken, however, and the Mandan readily agreed to the Americans' building a lodge.

The work of building the lodge was carried out under difficult circumstances. There was plenty of wood in the area, and the Corps of Discovery included several good carpenters, but the building materials had to be brought from a distance, sometimes from across the Missouri, and the winter cold was growing in intensity. As Clark described it, he and Captain Lewis moved into their "hut" on November 20, 1804, just in time.

The Long Winter

Even in the twenty-first century, states such as North Dakota and Minnesota report some of the coldest weather in the United States. In Lewis and Clark's time, temperatures were much worse. One of the lowest recorded temperatures was on December 12, 1804, when Clark recorded:

> Clear cold morning wind from the north, the thermometer at sun rise stood at 38 degrees below 0, moderated until 6 o'clock at which time it began to get colder. I line my gloves and have a cap made of the skin of the *Louservia* [Lynx or wild cat of the north] the fur near 3 inches long.

Living Indoors

The temperatures that Clark recorded at Fort Mandan that winter—anywhere from 20 degrees above to 40 degrees below zero Fahrenheit—are so severe that we might imagine the Corps of

Discovery staying inside all the time. To the contrary, the men found it necessary to be out and about much of the time.

There was wood to be cut and boats to be maintained. Some of the boats were stuck in the frozen river. Men had to stand guard duty and keep fires going around the clock. Because the Corps of Discovery was filled with men of large appetites, hunting parties had to go out in search of deer, fox, and other game.

Captain Lewis went on his first buffalo hunt with men of the Mandan tribe on December 9. Captain Clark made his first buffalo hunt on December 14. Both captains were experienced horsemen, but they were astonished at the speed with which the Mandan rode. The Mandan were better horsemen than any Virginia gentleman. Lewis's hunting party was the more successful; he returned with nine buffalo.

Despite the weather and the workload, there was time for pleasantry. Lewis and Clark entertained a number of Mandan and Blackfeet chiefs during the winter, and the men of the corps socialized with members of the local tribes. There also were visits from a handful of Englishmen who were employees of the Hudson's Bay Company and the Northwest Company (fur trapping companies which, at one time, owned almost as much land as the government of Canada). The Europeans dropped in to check up on the interloping Americans. Lewis and Clark stayed on good terms with the English visitors but were prepared, if necessary, to order them out of the area, which they now claimed as part of the United States.

New Year's Day of 1805 brought some much-needed entertainment. Clark awoke to the sound of two cannons firing, and he permitted 16 members of the Corps of Discovery to visit nearby Mandan settlements to sing and dance for the American Indians. To Clark's surprise, his black slave, York, was the biggest hit of all.

Sadly, there is no account of what York thought about being the subject of so much interest. He was the first black person the Mandan had ever seen.

New Year's Day in what today is North Dakota was unseasonably warm that year: The temperature reached 34 degrees above zero. It began to snow the next day, however. The Corps of Discovery was in for a real Midwestern winter.

ARTISTS AND INDIANS

When he planned the expedition of the Corps of Discovery, President Jefferson thought of almost everything: maps, compasses, and gifts for the American Indians. Modern-day Americans can gain a great appreciation of the exploits of Lewis and Clark through reading their journals. Many readers would be even more delighted, however, if an artist had made sketches or watercolor paintings of the American Indians the explorers met and the world in which they lived. Happily, artists later filled that gap.

Lewis and Clark on the Lower Columbia River painted by Charles M. Russell.

Tribal Warfare

Worse than the weather was the Sioux tribe. Lewis and Clark had left them behind in late September, but the Sioux knew where the Corps of Discovery was spending the winter.

The artist George Catlin was born in Pennsylvania in 1796. Between 1830 and 1836, he made five trips from St. Louis, Missouri, to the upper reaches of the Missouri River. Fascinated by the American Indians who lived in that region—the Mandan especially—he painted many of them. A few of the chiefs whom Catlin painted had been alive at the time that Lewis and Clark came through, 30 years before. Catlin's depiction of York, William Clark's African-American slave, meeting the Mandan, is considered one of the best representations of the Lewis and Clark expedition.

Karl Bodmer was born in Switzerland. He traveled across the Atlantic as the watercolor artist of Prince Maximilian of Germany, who led an expedition almost 5,000 miles up and down the Missouri River between 1833 and 1834. Like George Catlin, Karl Bodmer was entranced by the American Indians and their way of life. His many paintings have a strongly romantic tinge. This suggests that, like many other Europeans, he saw the American West through idealistic, rose-tinted eyeglasses.

Unlike Catlin and Bodmer, Charles Russell was a true son of the frontier. Born in Missouri in 1864, he moved to Montana around 1880 and lived as a cowboy on the range for many years. Because of this, he painted with more knowledge and understanding than either of his predecessors. Russell also was concerned about the disappearance of the old ways of life on the Great Plains: He composed many of his paintings so that future Americans could see what the Old West looked like.

Starting around 1900, Russell became fascinated with Lewis and Clark. He painted many scenes of their great expedition, including one that showed the reunion of Sacagawea and her childhood friend Jumping Fish. His largest painting, and the one that is most connected with Lewis and Clark, is a huge watercolor entitled *Lewis and Clark Meeting the Flatheads at Ross' Hole*. The painting is 25 feet wide and 12 feet high. Russell died at Great Falls, Montana, in 1926.

None of these artists accompanied Lewis and Clark, but the vividly colored images they painted give us the best glimpse we have of what the land and its peoples might have looked like during the time of the two great explorers' expedition.

When the Corps of Discovery reached present-day North Dakota, they encountered the Mandan, one of the American Indian tribes of the area. Because travel during the winter months would have been impossible on the Missouri River, Lewis, Clark, and their men built a fort nearby and named it after their new friends: Fort Mandan *(above)*.

In November, the Sioux attacked the Arikara Indians, both to try to show who was boss in the region and to punish the Lewis and Clark expedition for slipping through their fingers two months before. Captain Clark went out immediately with a detachment of men. Clark did not catch the Sioux, but he chased them well out of the Arikara neighborhood.

In February, the Sioux came back. This time, they preyed on four members of the Corps of Discovery who were bringing much-needed meat to Fort Mandan. The Sioux did not kill or harm the four men, but they took much of the meat.

This time, Captain Lewis went in search of the Sioux. He and some Mandan allies marched nearly 40 miles through frigid conditions in pursuit, but Lewis and the Mandan, like Captain Clark before them, came up empty. When he returned to Fort Mandan, Captain Lewis became much stricter about matters of defense; the men were kept on continuous alert. Sometimes, Lewis's zeal went to extremes. He nearly had a man given 50 lashes simply for climbing over the fort's palisade fence. By doing so, the man showed a nearby American Indian how it could be done—a possibly fatal breach of security. The court-martial sentenced the man to 50 lashes but recommended mercy. Lewis withdrew the punishment.

New Members of the Corps

During the winter of 1804–1805, Lewis and Clark befriended a French-Canadian fur trapper who showed skill with a hunting rifle and also knew American Indian languages. Toussaint Charbonneau was born near Quebec, in Canada, in 1767. He spent most of his adult life in the western Great Lakes area, and he knew the American Indians better than any other non-Indian the captains had met so far. Charbonneau readily agreed to join the expedition as an interpreter. He also mentioned that he wished to bring one of his American-Indian wives along. The captains agreed that he could bring one, but not both, of his two wives. Charbonneau selected 16- or 17-year-old Sacagawea, whose name meant Bird Woman. A Shoshone, she had been captured by the Blackfeet about five years before and had been transferred from one owner to another until she came to Charbonneau. Technically, she was his slave.

Lewis and Clark found Sacagawea agreeable. She gave birth in February, with Captain Lewis acting as midwife, and the captains permitted Sacagawea and Charbonneau to bring their new son with them on the journey. The baby's name was Jean Baptiste.

The Approach of Spring

As the days lengthened and the cold receded, the members of the Corps of Discovery were eager to be on the move. Lewis and Clark were no less anxious than the others, but they had many tasks to accomplish before they continued westward. One of the first, and most important, of these tasks was to send materials back to President Jefferson. That way, if the members of the corps did not return, at least there would be a record of their doings.

Lewis and Clark spent the better part of a month assembling, arranging, and cataloguing the specimens they had collected since leaving St. Louis. Some seemed trivial, such as pebbles from different rivers; others, such as Captain Clark's big map, seemed of greater import. Whatever its relative importance, Lewis and Clark assigned a place and a number to every item. Eventually, the men produced a journal that ran to 45,000 words and collected box upon box of carefully sorted specimens.

Then, too, there was the question of who should continue on the journey and who should return to St. Louis. Almost all of the men wished to be part of the ongoing group. Lewis and Clark eventually chose a few men to return east. Among them was John Newman, a corps member who had been court-martialed for insubordination the previous autumn. Since then his conduct had been exemplary, yet this was not enough to remove the stain on his record, and Lewis and Clark decided to send him back.

Lewis wrote a long letter to President Jefferson in which he praised the natural beauty of the region and described its potential benefits to the United States. Of the men with whom he would continue on the journey, Thwaites' *Journals* records that he wrote:

> At this moment, every individual of the party are in good health, and excellent spirits; zealously attached to the enterprise, and anxious to proceed; not a whisper of discontent or murmur is to be heard among them; but all in unison, act with the most perfect harmony. With such men I have everything to hope, and but little to fear.

Rivers, Mountains, and Bears

THE CORPS OF DISCOVERY SEPARATED ON APRIL 7, 1805. SIX members headed back for St. Louis, carrying all sorts of maps, journal records, and animal samples on the big keelboat.

Captain Clark recorded the names of those who continued westward:

Sergeant Nathaniel Pryor, Sergeant John Ordway, Sergeant Patrick Gass, [Private] William Bratten, John Colter, Joseph and Reuben Fields [brothers], John Shields, George Gibson, George Shannon, John Potts, John Collins, Joseph Whitehouse, Richard Windser, Alexander Willard, Hugh Hall, Silas Gutrich, Robert Frazure, Peter Crouzat, John Baptise Le Page, Francis Labich, Hugh McNeal, William Warner, Thomas P. Howard, Peter Wiser, J.B. Thompson, and my servant York, George Drewyer who acts as hunter & interpreter, Charbonneau and his Indian [wife] to act as interpreter and interpretess for the Snake [Shoshone] Indians—one Mandan & Charbonneau's infant.

Three new crew members joined Lewis and Clark's expedition at Fort Mandan: Toussaint Charbonneau, his Shoshone wife Sacagawea, and their two-month-old son, Jean Baptiste. At winter's end, this small family and the Corps of Discovery began their journey toward the Rocky Mountains.

Thirty-two persons plus the two captains came to 34 in all. These were the men, one woman, and one two-month-old baby who now headed for the Rocky Mountains.

Heading West

The Missouri River now took the Corps of Discovery due west on a more regular course than the one the explorers had navigated during the previous year. The river's current had not lost its force, however, and the dangers of travel had not lessened. If anything, the dangers had increased, largely because of the presence of the grizzly bear in the region.

A British Canadian had been the first European explorer to see a grizzly bear, more than a century earlier, but few reports of the creature had reached the East Coast. In their journals, Lewis and Clark referred to the "white" or "grizzled" bear. Although the American Indians had given them numerous warnings about such bears, the captains did not seem very frightened. According to Lewis, who had not yet seen a grizzly bear, American Indians equipped with only bows and arrows or poor-quality muskets might fear a bear, but Virginians equipped with Kentucky rifles would not.

He was wrong.

The Corps of Discovery met its first grizzly in May, soon after it reached the confluence of the Yellowstone and Missouri rivers—the point at which the two rivers came together. Lewis and one other hunter killed that first bear with considerable difficulty. The second grizzly the explorers met proved to be both enormous and unyielding. It attacked and attacked again, even though six men, all armed with the best rifles, fired repeatedly at it. When the animal finally died, Lewis examined it. He decided that it weighed about 600 pounds. He also noted that there were nine bullets in its carcass. As he later wrote, "the curiosity of the party is pretty well satisfied" on the subject of the grizzly bear. From then on, the Corps of Discovery tried to avoid battles with grizzly bears.

By the time the expedition reached the Yellowstone River, Lewis and Clark felt rather confident about their direction and the possibilities for success. Long talks with the Mandan and the Blackfeet during the winter had persuaded the explorers that the sources of the Yellowstone and Missouri rivers were close to one another. This was, in fact, the case. Their winter talks with the Mandan and Blackfeet also had convinced the captains that the source of the Columbia River, which ran to the Pacific, was only half a day's march from the sources of the other two rivers. This notion was completely wrong. Lewis and Clark did not comprehend the great size and breadth of the Rocky Mountains.

Leaving the area in which the Yellowstone and Missouri rivers flowed together, Lewis and Clark led the expedition westward. They were searching for a river that the Mandan called "the river that scolds at all others." The captains thought that this great stream might connect with the Saskatchewan River to the north.

Then, on May 26, Lewis had his first look at the Rocky Mountains. They still were far in the distance, but he could make out snow on their peaks, an indication that winter lingered much

FOUR RANGES DEEP

Even the most casual and inattentive traveler cannot help noticing the Rocky Mountains. A person who comes from the east by train sees the Rockies from hundreds of miles away. To someone who flies over them, these mountains seem to be a miracle of nature—which, indeed, they are.

Lewis and Clark knew the Appalachian Mountains well, and they believed that their experiences in those eastern mountains would serve them well as they crossed the Rockies. There is little in common between the two sets of mountain ranges, however. The Appalachians are older than the Rockies, and their greater age has allowed for greater erosion. This erosion has brought down the Appalachians' height. The Appalachians vary in height from 2,000 feet to 4,000 feet, and the mountain system features many valleys and hillsides. The Rockies, in contrast, vary from 8,000 feet to 12,000 feet in height. Even so, if it were only a matter of the Rockies' greater height, the Corps of Discovery might have had an easier time. The real trouble was in the Rockies' greater depth.

The Rockies are a single mountain chain that is made up of numerous ranges. Climbers can ascend the top of what seems to be the tallest peak, only to find before them a large valley, beyond which are even higher peaks. In some places, the Rockies have four ranges.

Lewis and Clark did not know this when they set out. They could not know it simply by looking at the Rockies from ground level. They learned about the Rockies' great depth and formidable breadth by trial and error—by walking through those mountains that, even today, can present fearsome challenges to travelers.

longer in the highlands. Lewis did not confide his anxiety to the men. There are indications in the journals, however, that he and Clark both were concerned about the height of these distant peaks.

On June 3, the corps came to a point at which the Missouri was joined by another river. The difficulty lay in knowing which stream was the Missouri.

As careful observers, Lewis and Clark determined that the stream that came in from the right—the northwest—was 200 yards across, and the stream that came in from the left—the southwest—was 372 yards across. Even this did not answer the question, however, because the stream that flowed from the northwest was muddier than the one from the southwest and, therefore, looked more like the Missouri.

Lewis and Clark spent almost three days scouting the area and exploring upstream on both rivers. They returned from their scouting convinced that the river that ran from the southwest was the true Missouri, and the one that ran from the northwest was a tributary. The trouble was that almost every other member of the Corps of Discovery believed that the captains were wrong.

The sergeants and privates of the corps believed that the fast-flowing river from the northwest was the Missouri, because of its muddy appearance. When the captains expressed their certainty, however, there was no argument. The men of the corps had come to believe in their captains. As if to prove their satisfaction with the captains, the men put on a special entertainment that evening, with Pierre Cruzatte playing merrily on his violin.

Lewis named the river that flowed from the northwest the Marias River, after a cousin of his in Virginia. Luckily for the corps, Lewis and Clark were correct. The true Missouri flowed into this meeting of waters from the southwest.

After leaving Fort Mandan, Lewis and Clark led their team west until they reached a fork in the Missouri River *(above)*. Unsure of which route to take, the group scouted the area before making a final decision, one that was not unanimous among the crew but nonetheless respected.

The Great Falls

During the winter, Lewis and Clark had heard various American Indians speak of the Great Falls of the Missouri. These falls, the speakers claimed, were unmatched in majesty. On June 13, Lewis was ashore, walking well in advance of the Corps of Discovery, when he heard a distant roar. It was music to his ears because it confirmed that he and Clark had been right about the Missouri and the Marias rivers. Even so, he was astonished by what he found:

The water after descending strikes against the abutment before mentioned, or that on which I stand, and seems to reverberate, and being met by the more impetuous current they roll and swell into half-formed billows of great height, which rise and again disappear in an instant. This abutment of rock defends a handsome little bottom of about three acres, which is diversified and agreeably shaded with some cottonwood trees.

After writing more than 1,000 words, Lewis expressed disgust with his feeble attempt. He stated that it was impossible to do justice to the Great Falls, which he said were equaled by only one other spectacle, that of the East's Niagara Falls. The thousands of tourists who have traveled this way in Lewis's footsteps have tended to agree with him: The majesty of the scene cannot be put into words.

Even as Lewis marveled at the beauty of the area, he knew that this natural wonder meant much work for the men. The Corps of Discovery had to portage—that is, carry—its canoes and equipment overland to a place beyond the falls. Additionally, Lewis had long desired to build a new and bigger boat in which to carry the expedition's journals, specimens, and other articles of importance. So, as most of the men of the party began the backbreaking task of portage, Lewis and a few others set about assembling what he called "the Experiment."

Back at Harpers Ferry, Virginia, as the expedition had been fitted out, Lewis had looked for a ready-made boat that could be carried in pieces and assembled at a future date. The best he could come up with was an iron-framed boat that used a sort of inflation system to pump up its outer skin. The whole thing was a failure, however.

Lewis experimented with coverings made of different types of wood and fur, and he tried different types of caulking devices to make the boat watertight, but everything he tried ended in failure. He spent more than a week on the project, but "the Experiment" would not stay afloat. Lewis gave up on his boat and turned his attention to what Clark and the others had been doing: hauling the party's seven canoes over a 25-mile stretch of land and water.

Portaging took skill. Many members of the Corps of Discovery had portaged in the past, but the Great Falls presented special difficulties. Not only was the distance long, but there also were all sorts of natural obstacles. Among these were the abundant prickly pear cactus plants, the spines of which pierced the men's moccasins. Some of the men complained about the situation. As the men struggled and became miserable, the captains worried. Lewis and Clark did not express their anxieties openly, but they both looked uneasily at the mountains, which now were close. There seemed to be no end to them, and they were covered with snow.

All the way from Fort Mandan, the Corps of Discovery had battled wind and sand that blew into the men's eyes. Now, as Lewis surveyed the mountains, he came up with what he believed to be the answer. From Thwaites' *Journals of Lewis and Clark*:

I think it possible that these almost perpetual S.W. winds proceed from the agency of the Snowy Mountains and the wide, level, and untimbered plains which stretch themselves along their bases for an immense distance, i.e. that the air coming in contact with the snow is suddenly chilled and condensed, thus becoming heavier than the air beneath in the plains.

Lewis's theory lacked some elements of the scientific truth, but it was amazingly accurate for the time. Once again, he showed himself to be a keen observer.

Into the Mountains

On July 24, the Corps of Discovery came to a place where the Missouri divided into three streams. The explorers named the three rivers the Jefferson, the Gallatin, and the Madison, after the president, the secretary of the treasury, and the secretary of state. Once again, the corps was confronted with a question of direction; and, once again, they chose correctly. Assisted by Sacagawea, who by now was seeing things that prompted her memory, the men chose the middle branch—the one they named the Jefferson—and headed for the Rocky Mountains.

The Jefferson became smaller and trickier as they traveled. Captain Clark led the main part of the corps through this area. Captain Lewis, meanwhile, was well out in front of the corps, moving on foot.

Meeting the Shoshone

Lewis and three other members of the corps were in the lead on August 11, when they caught sight of the first American Indian they had seen since leaving Fort Mandan. The man turned out to be a Shoshone, but he galloped away when Lewis came within 100 yards. Upset by this missed opportunity, Lewis "felt quite as much mortification [embarrassment] and disappointment as I had pleasure and expectation at the first sight of this Indian." Lewis's disappointment soon was forgotten when he and the other three men realized that they had achieved a major objective. In the middle of Lemhi Pass, on the border between present-day Montana and Idaho, they at last reached the source of the Missouri River. Ever since the expedition had set out, on

May 14, 1804, the fortunes of the Corps of Discovery had been tied to the Big Muddy. Now, for the first time, the men were about to try their luck on another river.

Lewis left the tiny stream that gave birth to the mighty Missouri and crossed Lemhi Pass. On the other side of the pass, he "first tasted the water of the great Columbia River." The stream that he found is now called Horseshoe Bend Creek. By following it first into the Beaverhead and Salmon rivers and then into the Snake River, a traveler can, indeed, find his or her way, eventually, to the Pacific Ocean. Lewis, however, still believed in a mistaken idea that had deceived the Corps of Discovery from the beginning. President Jefferson wanted

THE NORTHWEST PASSAGE

To find the Northwest Passage was a seafarer's dream. Such a passage would allow ships to sail westward from ports in northern Europe, across the North Atlantic and all the way to the Pacific, without having to travel southward through the Caribbean Sea and around the southern tip of South America. The idea had been around at least since 1497, when England's King Henry VII sent explorer John Cabot on a westbound voyage of discovery. In the age of England's Queen Elizabeth I, hardy captains such as Sir Martin Frobisher and Sir Francis Drake also sought the Northwest Passage.

Drake was the second man to sail around the world (between 1577 and 1580). Also in the 1570s, Frobisher became one of the first Europeans to explore the area of Hudson's Bay, in the Canadian Arctic. Neither man found the passage, however. Another Englishman, Henry Hudson, who sailed under the Dutch flag, lost his life in the bay that bears his name as he searched for the passage.

the explorers to look for a Northwest Passage—a water route all the way across North America, from the Atlantic Ocean to the Pacific. Lewis and Clark had become convinced that it was merely a short passage—perhaps a half-day's trek—to the shores of the Pacific Ocean from the point at which the rivers that flowed into the Missouri met the rivers that flowed into the Pacific.

On August 12, Lewis met the Shoshone. He befriended Chief Cameahwait, whose name means "He who never walks," but the two men were unable to communicate effectively until Sacagawea arrived. These were her people, the tribe from whom she had been stolen five years earlier. Her return allowed for

When the Scottish-Canadian Alexander Mackenzie became the first European explorer to cross the northern part of the North American continent by land, in 1793, he, too, had been searching for a passage. A few years later, in the early years of the nineteenth century, President Thomas Jefferson hoped that an all-water route, broken only by a short portage across the mountains of the American West, would give the United States what England and Canada had failed to find. Lewis and Clark allowed themselves to be deceived into this hope; in the winter of 1804–1805, the American Indians had suggested to the leaders of the Corps of Discovery that it was not a great distance from the headwaters of the Missouri River to the headwaters of the Columbia.

The hope, of course, was in vain. There was no Northwest Passage. This became clear after Lewis and Clark's journals were published in 1814. Modern science and the study of climate change has discovered something startling, however. Early in the twenty-first century, because of the melting of the North Polar ice cap, it became possible, for the first time, for a ship to sail from the Atlantic, across the top of Canada, through the Bering Strait, and into the Pacific. In a strange way, the Northwest Passage finally has been found.

While scouting ahead of the expedition team with two other men, Lewis had his first encounter with the Shoshone *(above)*. Though he was able to communicate with them using basic sign language he learned from other American Indians, Lewis had to wait several days before Sacagawea and Charbonneau arrived to translate for the crew.

more detailed communication between Lewis and Clark and Cameahwait. It seemed, at last, with the help of the Shoshone, that the Corps of Discovery had a good chance to get over and through the Rocky Mountains.

Heights and Valleys

LEWIS, CLARK, AND THE CORPS OF DISCOVERY STAYED WITH Cameahwait and the Shoshone for more than a week. During that time, the explorers purchased more than 30 horses. Lewis and Clark found that the Shoshone were knowledgeable traders. The travelers may have had to pay more for the horses than they wished, but the animals were vital to the expedition's success.

Old Toby

Cameahwait and the Shoshone were anxious to leave the mountains to hunt buffalo on the northern plains; they planned to travel in the direction from which Lewis and Clark had just come. Thus, at the beginning of September, the Corps of Discovery headed northwest, and Cameahwait and the Shoshone headed southeast. One Shoshone man, an old warrior whom Lewis and Clark nicknamed "Old Toby," agreed to go with them to act as their guide. By now, Lewis and Clark were quite anxious, both about the height of the mountains and the coming of winter.

Old Toby guided the Corps of Discovery northward, into the Bitterroot Valley, on the modern border of Montana and Idaho. The Shoshone guide knew the region well, but the maps that he drew and the remarks that he made did not always comfort the captains. Old Toby seemed certain that the corps would get through the mountains in a matter of days. All the travelers saw, however, were towering peaks covered with snow.

On September 4, 1805, Lewis and Clark met a large group of Nez Perce ("Pierced Nose") Indians. There were about 400 men, women, and children in the group, which also had about 500 horses. The captains found the Nez Perce to be willing traders, and quite a few horses were exchanged or sold during the explorers' two-day stay in the area. The corps then moved on, further into the Bitterroot Valley.

Clark's journal entries indicate the increasing anxiety of the captains:

September 8. . . . Proceeded on down the valley, which is poor stony land . . .

September 9. . . . The stream appears navigable, but from the circumstance of their being no salmon in it I believe there must be a considerable fall in it below . . .

September 13. . . . My guide took a wrong road and took us out of our route 3 miles through an intolerable route . . .

After they left the Bitterroot Valley, the corps climbed up the western side of the Bitterroot Mountains. There, they found cold, snow, and an overpowering sense of being lost. Worst of all, there was almost no game in the region, and the travelers grew increasingly hungry. According to Thwaites' *Journals*, Monday, September 16, was the worst day of all:

> *Knobs, steep hillsides and fallen timber continue today, and a thickly timbered country of eight different kinds of pine, which are so covered with snow that in passing through them we are continually covered with snow. I have been wet and as cold in every part as I ever was in my life.*

As bad as things were, the corps could not turn back. It would take too long to return to the point from which they first entered the mountains. Their only hope was to forge onward. On September 18, the men ate their last kernels of corn. There was no food remaining. Captain Clark went on ahead in the hope of finding something to eat.

Then, just when all seemed hopeless, the party came to a break in the mountains, and Captain Lewis could see an expanse of open prairie to the west. Although this prairie appeared to be about 60 miles away, Old Toby assured Lewis that they would reach it in a day or two. Hours later, the corps came upon a deer that Captain Clark had killed and left hanging in a tree; it was the first fresh meat they had seen in some time. By September 23, all members of the corps had stumbled out of the Bitterroot Mountains and onto the prairie of what today is eastern Washington State. They had made what historian Stephen Ambrose's *Undaunted Courage* called "one of the great forced marches of American history."

Horses and Dogs

Lewis and Clark and their company had come out of an area of North America (the northern Rockies) in which the American Indian groups were among the continent's most materially impoverished, into an area (the Pacific Northwest) where the tribes were among the richest in resources. From here on, the tribal peoples the explorers met tended to be rich in fish, timber, and fresh game. The Corps of Discovery also was astonished to see how plentiful dogs were among these native peoples.

The first meeting with American Indians of the Pacific Northwest was a mixed blessing, however. The members of the corps gorged themselves on the suddenly abundant food, and many, including Captain Lewis, became ill. Captain Clark had to shoulder nearly all the responsibilities of captaincy for a week. Clark tended his fellow captain and many of the men in their illness and also led the way in hollowing out six dugout canoes for what he hoped would be the last stage of their long journey to the Pacific. Clark had observed the Nez Perce method of burning out logs to make canoes, and he followed their example. By October 5, the Corps of Discovery had enough canoes to float themselves and their baggage down the Clearwater River.

Water Travel

Much of the journey that the Corps of Discovery had accomplished thus far had been made uphill, whether ascending into the mountains or paddling against the current of the mighty Missouri River. Now, for almost the first time since they left St. Louis, the members of the corps felt a river's current behind them, helping them on their way. They made better progress than at any previous time. The explorers did not speak much about the dangers through which they had passed, but anyone who cared to look over his (or her) shoulder could see the towering peaks of the Rockies and thank God that they had come this far.

Old Toby, the Shoshone guide who brought them through the Bitterroot Mountains, disappeared on the evening of October 8. Perhaps he was afraid of the American Indian tribes that

Both Lewis and Clark kept extensive diaries, but it was Clark who continued to write throughout the entire journey. Filled with sketches of plants and animals, Clark's diary included detailed information he received from local American Indians along with his maps and observations. Clark, who was mainly schooled at home by a tutor, made many spelling and grammar errors, but his diary remains the best account of the expedition.

the party would meet along the way. In any case, Old Toby left without taking any pay for his efforts. Lewis and Clark wanted to send a horseman after him with his pay. Two Nez Perce chiefs had been accompanying the expedition. They assured Lewis and Clark that any pay would be stripped from the guide as he passed through Nez Perce lands. Old Toby did take two horses at the Nez Perce camp when he rode off, however, and neither he nor the horses were seen again.

For some reason, at about this time, Captain Lewis stopped writing in his journal. To this day, we do not know why. All the entries for the autumn of 1805 come from the pen of Captain Clark. He was not as thorough an observer as Lewis, and his descriptions of the American Indians met along the way are not as full. Readers of Clark's entries still feel the presence of a remarkably skillful man, however.

LEWIS AND CLARK AND THE AMERICAN INDIANS

Normally, the Corps of Discovery was honest and fair in its dealings with American Indians. Knowing that the corps represented the advance wave of increasing numbers of American settlers, Lewis and Clark made every effort to win American Indians over to them. There were some exceptions to this general rule, however.

As they left the mountains and entered the Columbia River valley, Lewis and Clark found the American Indians of the region less welcoming than those of the Rockies. Items and animals around the explorers' campsite began to disappear. At first, Lewis and Clark reacted to these disappearances with self control. When the captains became angry, however, their response was out of proportion to the offense. Lewis nearly started a conflict with one tribe when his dog, Seaman, went missing.

The Corps of Discovery was responsible for some disappearances of its own. On the night of October 14, 1805, as they headed down the Columbia, the men of the corps helped themselves to some wood on an island, thus breaking one of their own rules. Later, in the spring of 1806, the explorers took an Indian canoe to add to their fleet.

Incidents such as these raise a question. Did Lewis and Clark see the American Indians as equals, as inhabitants and fellow guardians of the lands through which the corps passed? The answer, unfortunately, seems to be no. Lewis and Clark thought of most of the American Indians they met as children of the man the captains referred to as the "Great Father" in Washington, D.C. The explorers felt an obligation to be even-handed, even generous, in their dealings with the American Indians, but it was the fairness that a superior—a parent, or teacher, or master— extended to an inferior.

Even Lewis and Clark, with their knowledge of the Missouri River, were surprised by the strength and force of the Columbia River rapids. That river ran at least twice as fast in 1805 as it does today, when its flow is slowed and controlled by massive dams. First, the corps had to get through the Great Falls of the Columbia, a task that required much portaging. The men then had to run what professionals today—people who grade the difficulty of rapids to advise kayakers and whitewater rafters—call a class five rapid. (A class five rapid is considered the most difficult and dangerous that can be run; a class six rapid is one that even most experts cannot run.) The men of the corps did this without losing a boat or person. The captains acknowledged that when it came to water travel, they had much to learn from the American Indians.

Lewis and Clark were wise enough to realize that because they climbed up so high into the Rocky Mountains, they had to face a sharp climb down on their way to the sea. This proved to be the case. On October 23, 1805, they started along a 55-mile stretch of the Columbia River that took them down, again and again, in descents through swirling whitewater. It was here that the captains led the men through a class five rapid. The explorers skillfully guided their dugout canoes through this danger zone.

Scents of the Sea

By the time the expedition reached what is now Portland, Oregon, Lewis and Clark were certain that the ocean was not far. They saw American Indians wearing items of clothing that indicated that the groups had traded with Europeans. (British sea captains had been coming to the area around the mouth of the Columbia River for about five years.)

Today, many people would love to be able to eat as much salmon as Lewis and Clark did. The captains and most of their company were heartily tired of the fish, however. They often traded with local tribes for dogs because the travelers much preferred dog meat to yet another meal of fish.

On November 2, the corps came to the confluence of the Sandy and Columbia rivers. This was the highest point on the Columbia River that any European had ever come. (An Englishman had reached the meeting of the rivers in 1792.) On the fifth day of the same month, Lewis and Clark encountered long, American Indian–built canoes—the first they had seen. Magnificently sculpted from wood, these coastal vessels made a strong impact on the men of the corps.

As they came closer to the ocean, Lewis and Clark noted their first sightings of totem poles. The explorers did not use that name for these carved columns, however; the term was invented much later. The men marveled at the beautiful and impressive woodwork but kept on. At last, on the afternoon of November 7, 1805, the goal of all of their travels—from Pittsburgh to St. Louis to the American Northwest—came into view. According to Thwaites' *Journals of Lewis and Clark*, Clark recorded a new entry: "A cloudy foggy morning, some rain. We set out early. . . . After delaying at this village one hour and a half we set out piloted by an Indian dressed in a sailor's dress, to the main channel of the river. . . ." Then, at some point in midafternoon, Clark looked up and saw an immense body of water. "Ocean, oh the joy!" he wrote.

Later that evening, with more time to collect his thoughts, Clark wrote, "Great joy in camp, we are in view of the Ocean, this great pacific Ocean which we have been so long anxious to see, and the roaring or noise made by its waves breaking on the rocky shores (as I suppose) may be heard distinctly. We made 34 miles today."

They had done it. No matter that they still were in the Columbia River estuary or that it would take 10 more days before they rounded the bay and truly saw the Pacific. After a year and a half of innumerable hardships, they had crossed the continent.

Fort Clatsop

The traveler who follows in Lewis and Clark's footsteps is rewarded at many spots, but most especially at the end of the transcontinental journey. The estuary of the Columbia River is as beautiful as it was in 1805, and the presence of humans is felt less here than in many other parts of the United States. Lewis, Clark, and their company did much sightseeing in their first 10 days in the area, but they then faced an important decision: where to spend the winter.

They could not head back during the winter months. The Rockies were forbidding in September; they would be devastating in December. The Corps of Discovery knew that it would have to spend the winter along the Pacific coast, but where?

Although Lewis and Clark had won the full confidence of their company during the course of the expedition, the captains now put things to a vote. There were three choices: They could remain where they were, on the north bank of the Columbia; they could journey up the Columbia to a point at which the weather might be warmer; or they could go to the south bank of the river and proceed from there.

The way the choices were proposed, it made sense that most members of the company voted for the last choice of the three; it was, after all, the most open-ended of the possibilities. Here the captains were of different minds, however. Lewis was all for the south bank. Clark, however, thought that salt water was bad for the health; he voted for the second choice, to go upstream on the Columbia. Sacagawea—who was given a vote—expressed her desire to be somewhere near the acacia roots on the south shore of the Columbia River. As Stephen Ambrose puts it in *Undaunted Courage*, York, the member of the expedition who was William Clark's slave, also voted. As Ambrose noted, "This was the first vote ever held in the Pacific Northwest. It was the first time in American history that a black slave had voted, the first time a woman had voted."

Like Fort Mandan before it, Fort Clatsop was built to shelter the Corps of Discovery and named after a local American-Indian tribe. The entire crew lived in the small house from December 1805–March 1806. Because much of the original structure had decayed since the fort was occupied, the National Park Service has constructed a replica of Fort Clatsop that is open to the public *(above)*.

The Corps of Discovery crossed to the south bank of the Columbia at a point above the estuary, which was simply too wide and dangerous to cross. The company then made its way down to the coast. Captain Lewis went ahead and marked the spot at which they would build Fort Clatsop, the structure to get them through the winter. As described in the expedition journals, the fort was built as a square, 50 feet long by 50 feet wide, with enough room inside for everyone.

Toward the end of the year, there came news that an enormous whale had washed ashore about 20 miles to the south. Hoping to obtain some blubber for the winter, Lewis and Clark planned to send men down the coast. The captains then learned that Sacagawea wanted to go, too. They said no at first, but she continued to ask, saying that she had never seen the ocean and that it was very hard for her to miss this opportunity. The captains relented. With this incident, Sacagawea makes her most notable vocal appearance in the journals. Most of the time, the captains referred to her non-descriptively in the third person; here she steps forward on the page.

With the fort built and enough elk to get the party through the cold season, the Corps of Discovery settled in for a winter on the Pacific Northwest.

Separation and Reunion

CAPTAIN LEWIS RESUMED HIS JOURNAL WRITING ON JANUARY 1, 1806: "This morning I was awoke at an early hour by the discharge of a volley of small arms, which were fired by our party in front of our quarters to usher in the New Year; this was the only mark of respect which we had it in our power to pay this celebrated day."

If Lewis thought about the previous year—and his temperament suggests that he might have—he probably marveled at how far he and his company had come. One year ago, the Corps of Discovery had been at Fort Mandan, on the Great Plains. In the months since, it had crossed the Rockies and found a water route from the mountains' western slopes to the Pacific.

Clark, the less introspective of the two captains, wrote: "This morning at Day we were saluted from the party without, wishing us a 'happy new year', a shout and discharge of their arms."

Practicalities

As at Fort Mandan the winter before, Lewis and Clark made sure that the men kept busy; the captains knew that enforced idleness could bring down morale. There was carpentry to be done, there were wood fires to be maintained and there were maps to be made. Captain Clark spent many hours working on his map, which became the first to show a series of ranges in the Rocky Mountains.

Lewis and Clark also had to keep the men from spending too much time with local American Indian women. Some men of the local Chinook tribe sent their teenage daughters to the fort thinking that the men might enjoy their company. Lewis and Clark were not prudes; they knew that the men had sexual interests. Because there had been cases of sexually transmitted diseases in the corps in the past, however, the captains made the men promise not to have sexual relations during the winter.

The winter of 1805–1806 was a profitable one in terms of natural history. President Jefferson had told Lewis and Clark the importance of recording and describing the natural wonders that they saw, including plants and animals. As they crossed the Great Plains and the Rockies, the captains became the first Americans to describe the grizzly bear and the prairie dog. Now, they became the first to record the plants and wildlife of the Pacific Northwest. As experienced woodsmen, Lewis and Clark gave much attention to the trees that they found:

Number 3, a species of fur, which one of my men informs me is precisely the same with that called the balsam fur of Canada. It grows here to considerable size, being from 2 and a half to 4 feet in diameter and rises to the height of 10 r 120 feet. Its stem is simple branching, ascending and proliferous [having leafy shoots growing from a flower or fruit]. Its leaves are sessile [flowers or leaves that grow directly from the stem], acerose [needlelike, like pine], one-eighth of an inch in length and one-sixteenth of an inch in width.

apparently jointed Consisting of 6 par and terminating in one (in this form.) Serrate, or like of a whip saw, each ... *sessile the teeth point terminating in a small subulate spine, being from 25 to 27 in numb, veins, smoth, plane and of a deep green, their points tending obliquely towards the extremity of the rib or common footstalk. I do not know the fruit or flower of either. the 1st. resembles a plant Common to many parts of the United States Called the Mountain Holly.—*

Tuesday February 13th 1806.

The Clatsop left us this morning at 11. A. m. not

As the first U.S. explorers to venture this far west, Lewis and Clark recorded sightings of animal, bird, and plant species previously unknown to them. *Above,* a drawing of an evergreen leaf in Clark's expedition diary.

It is easy to see why Lewis and Clark have been called two of America's early naturalists. In their journals, they often devoted more attention to plants and wildlife than to the harshness of the winters.

As they thought of home, which seemed a very long way, Lewis and Clark wondered whether they might catch a ship back to the United States. Using information supplied by the local American Indians, the explorers made a list of the sea captains whose ships came to this region. There were 12 names on the list, and some ships came every three months or so. Lewis and Clark decided not to depend on the likelihood of a sea voyage home, however.

Heading Home

The men of the corps built canoes—and stole one from the local American Indians, much to the corps's shame. The men also preserved and stored food. Lewis and Clark were eager to set off for home, but they realized that it made no sense to approach the Rocky Mountains until the winter snows had melted.

Finally, on March 20, 1806, the Corps of Discovery set its canoes into the water. Brandt's *Journals of Lewis and Clark* notes that the explorers had this to say about their winter home: "Although we have not fared sumptuously this winter and spring at Fort Clatsop, we have lived as comfortably as we had any reason to expect we should; and have accomplished every object which induced our remaining at this place except that of meeting with the traders who visit the entrance of the river."

As they headed up the Columbia on their return journey, the men looked back with few regrets. The Columbia River estuary was, indeed, the focus of their hopes and the goal of the expedition. They had found it a cold, damp place in which to spend the winter, however. Some of them even looked forward to the Rockies as a suitable change.

Retracing their passage was easy in that they now knew the way. It was difficult, however, in that they now paddled against the current. It was like being on the Missouri all over again, as the Corps of Discovery made slow progress against a swiftly running river.

Lewis and Clark met many of the same American Indians as they had the previous autumn. By now, the chiefs of the Columbia River valley were used to receiving medals from the American captains. (One chief still had his medal as late as 1855.) Lewis and Clark had to be careful about what they gave away at this point, however, because their supplies—of medals, of clothing, and of ammunition—were running low.

Moving slowly upstream was rewarding in one respect: The captains could study and evaluate the countryside with much greater leisure. What they saw was a vast, unspoiled region.

Even today, the Columbia and Snake river basins are among the wilder areas of the United States. In the time of Lewis and Clark, those rivers ran with much greater force as they carved their paths to the ocean. Many American Indians lived and hunted in the region, and Lewis and Clark did their best to compose a brief vocabulary of each tribal language. All was not peaceful, however; the Corps of Discovery found that some members of the river tribes were inclined, as before, to make off with small items. On one occasion, Captain Lewis almost came to blows with two American Indians; luckily, Captain Clark intervened.

There were a few days on which the corps could not make progress against the wind and the river current, both of which came from the far-off Rocky Mountains. On April 8, Lewis wrote: "The wind blew so violently this morning that we were obliged to unload [our] prigies [pirogues, a type of boat used by Lewis and Clark] and canoes, soon after which they filled with water. Being compelled to remain during the day at our present station, we sent out some hunters in order to add something to our stock of provisions."

The journal records that the hunters returned with "a duck only," but the corps was living better than it had in the past. The men now ate a more balanced diet. It consisted of salmon, the meat from various animals, and roots. With the amount of Omega-3 fatty acids in those foods, people of the twenty-first century might admire such a diet. The men of the Corps of Discovery found it tedious, however. Clearly lacking in the explorers' diet was a good source of green vegetables, and this was not remedied during the spring season.

Into the Mountains

The Corps of Discovery did not rush on the homeward trip. Lewis and Clark knew that it would be foolish to enter the Rocky Mountains early in the spring, so the corps maintained a leisurely pace as they passed through the land of the Nez Perce. The explorers found the two Nez Perce chiefs who had accompanied the corps for part of the way during the autumn, and Lewis and Clark once again asked them to be good friends and subjects of the president of the United States. The extent to which the chiefs agreed to—or even understood—this request is difficult to say. Historians and ethnologists (scientists who study peoples and their cultures) in the late-nineteenth century found many folk tales among the Nez Perce that told of Lewis and Clark. Evidently, the captains made quite an impression.

By mid-May, the corps reached the lower ranges of the Rocky Mountains. The explorers came up the Clearwater River and anticipated being able to cross the Bitterroot Mountains in May. They found, however, that the snows still were too deep. When they made the same attempt in June, they again found the mountains full of snow. In his journal, Captain Clark confided his fear of those mountains, which were so much larger than any that he or Lewis had known in eastern North America. There was no choice, however; the corps had to go on.

Fortunately, the Corps of Discovery had Nez Perce guides for its springtime move into the Bitterroot Mountains. The going was difficult, with much snow on the ground, but Captain Lewis wrote that the snow was sometimes beneficial because it made it easier for the horses to travel over natural obstacles.

The Bitterroots

These mountains had marked the toughest part of the westward journey. They did the same on the homeward leg. Game was scarce, and the snow was seven-feet deep in some places. There

In spite of everything they had experienced on their journey into the West, the Corps of Discovery was sorely tested again on their way home through the Bitterroot Mountains (*above*). Part of the larger Rocky Mountains, Lewis and Clark led their team through the area that bridges present-day Idaho and Montana with the help of Nez Perce guides.

were times when Lewis and Clark wrote in their journals with a sense of despair. The mountains seemed to go on forever: Would they ever get through?

Thanks to the Nez Perce guides, they did. At the beginning of July 1806, Lewis, Clark, and their company could see the end of the Bitterroots and some openings to the plains below. They had made it through the worst part of the journey.

On July 3, the Corps of Discovery split up. Wisely, Lewis and Clark had kept the corps together all the way to the Pacific and to this point on the return journey. Now, however, there was some extra exploring to do. Lewis and Clark remembered that a Shoshone named Twisted Hair had told them that it was an easy five-day journey from the eastern side of the Bitterroots to the Falls of the Missouri. Because it had taken them 56 days to come the other way, through Lemhi Pass and the Gates of the Mountains, Lewis and Clark felt that they must investigate this possible shortcut.

The captains decided to divide the corps into two groups. Captain Lewis and about six men would try to find this five-day passage and then ascend the Marias River, the one about which they had deliberated in August 1805. At the same time, Captain Clark would lead the other members of the corps down to the watershed of the Yellowstone River and follow it to its confluence with the Missouri. Whichever captain reached that meeting place first would wait for the other. The entire corps would then descend as one on the rest of the way home.

On paper and in the captains' minds, this was a perfectly sound plan. The best-laid plans of men often are defeated by the whims of nature, however.

Clark and Company

Clark's larger party was aided greatly by Sacagawea, who knew this area from her childhood days. Time and again, she pointed the better way for the corps. Because of her knowledge, the corps avoided the Lolo Trail, which had been a heartbreaking part of the westward journey. The company made its way down to a cache of supplies and canoes that the corps had left at the head of the Gallatin River the previous year. Happily, all the materials were still there.

Leaving most of their horses behind, Clark and his company boarded canoes and descended the Gallatin. The party then headed overland to the Yellowstone River. There, another separation of the corps took place. According to earlier plans, Clark detached four men to scout the Jefferson River as it ran to the Yellowstone and then to rendezvous with both himself and

Captain Lewis at the meeting of the Yellowstone and Missouri rivers. There was nothing wrong with the plan, but it called for nearly perfect coordination among three separate groups of men.

When Clark and his group reached the Yellowstone, he began one of the best parts of the entire journey of exploration. The men built canoes, put them in the fast-flowing water, and made incredible speed as they headed down the river. On one occasion, they traveled 80 miles in a single day. To men who had labored up the Missouri during the previous summer, to race down the Yellowstone was a joy. Speed did have its dangers, however; Clark's canoe nearly was overturned. In the end, everyone made it, safe and dry, to the meeting of the Yellowstone and Missouri rivers. At this point, the biggest enemies of Clark's group were swarms of mosquitoes. The attacks were so bad that Clark and his company chose to wait for Lewis downriver at the Missouri, a little past the actual confluence. The party posted a letter on a tree to alert Lewis to its location.

A few days later, the men who had gone down the Jefferson River arrived. With this reunion, the Corps of Discovery now was in two parts. Where, however, was Captain Lewis?

Lewis and Company

As he descended the east side of the Rockies, Captain Lewis must have felt a great sense of achievement—and of relief. Although he and Captain Clark were co-leaders of the expedition, President Jefferson had written the original commission to Lewis alone, and Lewis felt most responsible for the expedition's failure or success.

There was one nagging feeling of failure. Jefferson and Lewis had shared the dream of finding an all-water route (or at least a water route that involved a minimum of portaging) to the Pacific. That dream had been shattered in the incredible heights and depths of the Rockies. Lewis still had one hope for success, however. If a fast-flowing river such as the Marias was found to originate at latitude near the 49th parallel, then the United States may be able to negotiate a land treaty with Great Britain or even claim it and still be in the competition for a water route to the Pacific.

The Corps of Discovery was already in two parts, but Lewis soon made it three. He divided his party into two groups, one to navigate down the Missouri River and the other to explore the Marias. Lewis, the brothers Joseph and Reuben Fields, Patrick Gass, and five others headed north on the Marias.

Something in Lewis changed almost as soon as his party headed north. In previous months, his journal had been full of entries about natural history and the animal life of the regions through which he passed. Now, however, as he ascends the Marias, the tone of his entries becomes forbidding. Lewis noted the change in the soil, as the land became less fertile. He also made frequent references to the gradual disappearance of the buffalo. The farther north he went, the fewer buffalo he found.

On about July 16, Lewis gave up his hope that the Marias would lead him near the 49th parallel. If it had, it would have extended the size of the United States at the expense of British Canada. Lewis named his most northward camp Camp Disappointment. From that point, he turned around and headed south along the Marias. He soon ran into a party of Blackfeet warriors.

When Lewis first sighted them, the Blackfeet were on a gentle rise. They had about 30 horses, half of which were saddled. Lewis had seven men with him; another, George Drewyer, was about a mile away. The Blackfeet saw Drewyer long before they realized that Lewis and company were coming from the other direction. Fearing that the Blackfeet might attack and kill Drewyer, Lewis attracted the warriors' attention to himself. According to the journal, "About this time they discovered us and appeared to run about in a very confused manner as if much alarmed. . . . I calculated on their number being nearly or quite equal to that of their horses, that our running would invite pursuit, as it would convince them that we were their enemies."

Lewis summoned up all his courage and walked slowly toward the Blackfeet. His men came with him to a point but then paused intentionally, and Lewis went on by himself to meet the leading warrior. The two men shook hands. Each then passed the other to greet the other's party. It was a cautious beginning, fraught with danger, but Lewis made it through unharmed.

George Drewyer soon rejoined the party. Although Lewis feared that there were other Blackfeet in the region, what took place that day was an equal meeting between the nine explorers and eight American Indians. The Blackfeet proved to be fond of smoking, and Lewis sat up with them until about ten that evening. With Drewyer acting as interpreter, Lewis told the Blackfeet what he had told to so many other tribes: that the Great Father in Washington, D.C., claimed this land, and that the Blackfeet must live in peace with their neighbors. The Blackfeet made no dramatic signs of displeasure, but they indicated to Lewis that they were part of a much larger war party. There were, they said, many other warriors only half a day's ride away. Despite his anxiety, Lewis slept soundly that night. He and the other members of his company had endured much in recent days.

The Final Hazards

"D_ _ _ you, let go of my gun!"

Meriwether Lewis awoke to these words on the morning of July 27, 1806.

First Blood

Lewis had stayed up late the night before, smoking tobacco with the Blackfeet. He also had stood the first watch of the night. When he finally went to sleep, he fell into a deep slumber. On hearing George Drewyer cry out these words, however, Lewis awoke in a flash.

Lewis looked around and saw confusion. The two Fields brothers were chasing two or three Blackfeet from the corpsmen's campsite. George Drewyer was wrestling with a warrior for possession of Drewyer's rifle. Lewis looked for his own rifle but found it gone. He pulled out his pistol and jumped to his feet.

The Lewis and Clark expedition were able to use gifts and the help of Sacagawea to prevent conflict with various American Indian tribes until they split up and encountered the Blackfeet. Battle-ready and powerful, the Blackfeet viewed Lewis's group as a threat to their dominance in the region and attempted to steal from the Corps of Discovery, resulting in Lewis shooting a member of the Blackfeet (*above*).

The fault, if there was any fault, was Joseph Fields's. Fields had stood the last watch of the night and had dozed off. Two Blackfeet had snuck up on him and had taken both his rifle and that of Drewyer. Fields had awakened, cried out, and gone in pursuit of the two Blackfeet. Joined by his brother, he was able to overtake the two thieves and retrieve the rifles. During the encounter, Joseph Fields struck one of the Blackfeet with his knife, which pierced the man's heart and killed him in less than a minute. It was the first death caused by the Corps of Discovery.

Lewis, by now, was in full pursuit of the warrior who had his rifle. Because Lewis and Drewyer overtook him so quickly, the man dropped the gun and ran off. At this point, Lewis wished to return to the campsite, but the disturbance was not finished.

When they saw that they had lost the fight for the rifles, the Blackfeet tried to run off the explorers' horses. Lewis and Drewyer pursued the horse thieves. When one warrior came straight at him, Lewis shot him dead from a distance of 30 paces. The Blackfeet then dispersed, and the weary and astonished Americans regrouped at the campsite.

None of the members of the corps were harmed, but they had had a terrible shock.

Ride like the Wind

Anthony Brandt's abridgement of Lewis and Clark's journals quotes Lewis's journal entry:

While the men [of the corps] were preparing the horses I put four shields and two bows and quivers of arrows, which they [the Blackfeet] had left on the fire, with sundry other articles; they left all their baggage at our mercy. They had but two guns and one of them they left. The others were armed with bows and arrows and eye-dags. The gun we took with us I also retook the [American] flag but left the medal about the neck of the dead man that they might be informed who we were.

Lewis and his men then rode like the wind.

Knowing that there was a large Blackfeet war party somewhere to the south, Lewis led his men, on horseback, south by southeast. Lewis hoped to reach the safety of the larger party on the Missouri. When some of Lewis's men proposed another route, Lewis scolded them. He told them that their lives, and the lives of their comrades back on the Marias, depended on their rejoining the main party with the greatest speed possible. Lewis and his men covered 63 miles that day. After a rest of an hour and a half, they covered another 20 miles under the cover of night. Lewis commented, "My Indian horse [one captured from the Blackfeet] carried me very well, in short much better than my own would have done, and leaves me with but little reason to complain of the robbery."

On the morning of July 28, the men rose early. They were bone weary and stiff from the hard ride of the day before. They had to saddle up and ride on, however. They made excellent speed in the morning and in midafternoon were delighted to hear the sound of rifle shots in the distance. The sounds turned out to be what they hoped: Shots from the group Lewis had left a few weeks ago, coming down the Missouri River.

Reunion

On their third day of paddling on the Missouri, the Lewis party judged that the mouth of the Yellowstone, and Captain Clark's party, were 86 miles away. Lewis announced his intention to get there by that evening. They did, only to find the note on the tree informing them that Clark and company had continued downstream to escape from the mosquitoes.

Lewis and company rejoined their fellows on the Missouri River, and the reunited group made haste down the Big Muddy. There was one more hazard to endure, however.

On August 11, Lewis went hunting with Pierre Cruzatte. Deer had been plentiful all along the trip, but the corps now was in elk country, and Lewis decided to make the most of this opportunity, according to Thwaites' *Journals of Lewis and Clark*:

I killed one and he [Cruzatte] wounded another. We reloaded our guns and took different routes through the thick willows in pursuit of the elk. I was in the act of firing on the elk a second time when a ball struck my left thigh about an inch below my hip joint [in other words, in the buttocks]. . . . I instantly supposed that Crouzat had shot me in mistake for an elk, as I was dressed in brown leather and he cannot see very well. Under this impression I called out to him, "D_ _ _ you, you have shot me."

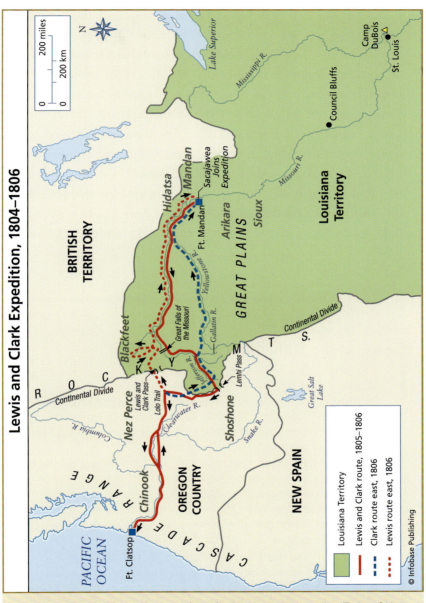

Lewis and Clark Expedition, 1804–1806

While waiting for the snow to melt in the Bitterroot Mountains, Twisted Hair, a member of the Nez Perce, told the group about a possible shortcut from the mountains to the Falls of the Missouri. Lewis and Clark, both believing there was more to see in the area, split up the Corps of Discovery into two groups in Montana and led them in different directions. After travelling on the Yellowstone and Marias rivers, the group was later reunited in present-day North Dakota.

Cruzatte had accidentally shot Lewis, and then disappeared into the woods (when asked about it later, Cruzatte denied having shot his leader). Lewis continued to call, but he received no response. Supposing that American Indians were about, he turned and ran—sometimes staggering because of his wound—all the way back to the canoes. Sergeant Gass helped Lewis out of his clothes, and Lewis cleaned and dressed the wound himself. Although there was no danger of Lewis's losing his life, it was an extremely painful situation.

On the next day, August 12, Lewis and his men caught up with Clark and his group, who had been waiting several days for Lewis to arrive. Clark immediately tended to Lewis's

WHAT HAPPENED BACK HOME?

The lives of the families of the men of the corps had changed little during the men's absence. The daily work of farming, carpentry, and other tasks went on as usual. The life of the nation had changed a good deal in two years and four months, however.

In the summer of 1804, as Lewis and Clark ascended the Missouri River, Vice President Aaron Burr and former secretary of the treasury Alexander Hamilton met at Weehawken, New Jersey, across the Hudson River from New York City, in a duel. Burr claimed that Hamilton had insulted his honor. Burr then demanded satisfaction, as the social code of dueling required.

It is said that Hamilton fired harmlessly into the air while Burr waited and that Burr then coolly shot Hamilton through the heart. Whatever the sequence of firing was, the former secretary of the treasury was dead, and the current vice president of the United States was about to be indicted for murder in two states, New York and New Jersey. Burr returned to Washington, D.C., and served out his term as vice president. He departed from the nation's capital in March 1805.

wound, which he described as more painful than severe. Interestingly, Lewis's contributions to the expedition journals stop on the day that he and his men made their rendezvous with Clark.

When Lewis and company caught up with Clark and company, the entire Corps of Discovery was at last reunited. Both Lewis and Clark's groups had experienced great adventures and dangers during their separation. Remarkably, neither group had lost a man.

From here on, it was all downhill, in a literal sense. The Missouri River tumbled on, mile after mile, and the men of the Corps of Discovery made their canoes fly down the Big Muddy.

At about the same time, the war between the United States and the Barbary pirates of Tripoli, in North Africa, came to an end. Tripoli had declared war on the United States in 1800, and President Jefferson had sent a naval force to subdue that city. As good as the United States Navy was, however, the American forces were unable to capture the city, and the Barbary War seemed destined to drag on forever. Finally, a Connecticut Yankee came to the rescue.

William Eaton was a Revolutionary War veteran. He came up with a creative idea. He planned to capture Tripoli by attacking not from the Mediterranean coast, but through Egypt, 800 miles to the east. Eaton arrived in Alexandria, Egypt, with a small group of U.S. Marines. He then led a remarkable march across the Libyan desert to surprise the enemy. It is this daring military action that is commemorated in the "Marines' Hymn" with the words, "to the shores of Tripoli." Tripoli sued for peace, and the war with the Barbary pirates came to an end.

Finally, and perhaps most importantly from President Jefferson's perspective, the British stepped up their impressments of American sailors. Between 1800 and 1810, about 5,000 Americans were seized, taken from their ships, and forced to serve in the British Navy. These shameless kidnappings helped to bring about the War of 1812 between Great Britain and the United States.

The men were weary from two years of travel, but they still put their backs into it. On some days they traveled 70 or 80 miles, and the landscape changed as they paddled through it. On Saturday, September 20, 1806, the Corps of Discovery came into the little settlement of La Charette, in what is now Missouri. This was the last outpost the explorers had passed, two years before, on their way west. On Sunday, September 21, they reached St. Charles, and on Monday, September 22, they were entertained by the people of that town. They reached their final destination on Tuesday, September 23: "We rose early. . . descended to the Mississippi and down that river to St. Louis, at which place we arrived about 12 o'clock. We suffered the party to fire off their pieces [guns] as a salute to the town. We were met by all the village and received a hearty welcome from its inhabitants."

Lewis, Clark, and all the members of the Corps of Discovery except for one (Sergeant Charles Floyd, who died in 1804) made it back to St. Louis after two-and-a-half years of travel. They were years filled with difficulties, obstacles, and periods of exhaustion. It was one of the great achievements in the history of exploration.

Home of the Heroes

Lewis and Clark had put hundreds of thousands of words into their journals, and they started to polish them almost as soon as they reached St. Louis. Even so, their joint report was not published for another eight years. In part, this was because there was so much else for the returned explorers to do.

Jefferson

President Jefferson was overjoyed to learn that Lewis and Clark and most of their men had returned safely. Although he had made no public comment, the president had just about given them up for dead.

The captains and their party received the royal treatment in the weeks that followed their return. First, on September 25, they were the guests of honor at a gala celebration at Christy's Inn, in St. Louis. Then, they were invited home to Virginia to receive the president's congratulations.

Lewis, Clark, a handful of their men, and several American Indians set out from St. Louis in November 1806. Captain Clark stopped at Louisville, where he intended to court Julia Hancock. Captain Lewis continued on and reached Charlottesville, Virginia, on December 15. After a lavish banquet there, Lewis and his party, which still included the American Indians, headed to Washington, D.C. Lewis arrived at the nation's capital three days before the end of the year.

President Jefferson received the American Indians on December 30 and 31. He met with Lewis on January 1. It was, beyond a doubt, an occasion for joy—but there was some mixture of disappointment, as well. Lewis and Clark had not found a water route to the Pacific. Instead, they became the first explorers to say that such a route might not exist. In one sense, then, the Corps of Discovery had failed. There was no Northwest Passage, at least not over the Rocky Mountains. The Far West was so much bigger, and the mountains were so much higher, than anyone had expected, that it was difficult to convey just how vast the land truly was.

Lewis did not disappoint President Jefferson. Jefferson's curiosity about natural history and the landscape of the West was as strong as ever. The biggest motivation for westward exploration—the hope of finding a Northwest Passage—was now laid to rest, however. While Lewis was in Washington, giving the president an eyewitness report of the Great West, Clark remained in the St. Louis area.

Reception

Lewis did not disappoint the general public, either. Most Americans knew little about Lewis and Clark in 1804, when they set out on their journey. By the beginning of 1807, however, their names had become household words. Tales abounded about the virtuous captains and their dutiful men.

In 1807, American poet Joel Barlow published "On the Discoveries of Lewis." After comparing Lewis to fellow ex-

WHAT HAPPENED TO THE MEN OF THE CORPS?

To the best of our knowledge, Sacagawea probably was the first to die, in 1812, at the age of about 25. Her son, Jean-Baptiste lived on for many years.

Sergeant Patrick Gass lived the longest; he died in 1870, at the age of 99.

John Ordway, who had many responsibilities during the trip, returned and married. He and his wife, Gracy, had no children. Both died in 1817.

George Drewyer died in a fight with the Blackfeet, not far from Cut Bank, Montana, where he and Lewis had fought with them in 1806.

Alexander Willard died in California in 1865. He and his wife, Eleanor, were photographed sometime in the 1860s; he is the only member of the Corps of Discovery whose photograph is available.

Much less is known about the other members of the expedition. One of the best records available to us comes from the pen of Captain Clark; in about 1828, he noted which members of the expedition were still alive. The saddest story, by far, is that of York, the expedition member who also was Clark's slave.

For most of two centuries, legend had it that Captain Clark freed York in recognition of his heroic actions during the expedition. In about 2000, however, it was learned that this was not true. After the return from the West, when Captain Clark moved from Kentucky to St. Louis, he and York had a quarrel. The argument was based on the fact that York's wife lived in Kentucky. The dispute became so intense that Clark did not want York around. Clark hired out his slave to other people. Eventually, perhaps around 1815, Clark did free York, but it was more the act of an exasperated owner than the gesture of a grateful friend. According to the best current knowledge, it is said that York owned several horses and that he went into business as a conveyor—a person who carried or forwarded freight. It is also said that the business failed, and that York died of cholera in Tennessee.

plorers Christopher Columbus and Alexander Mackenzie, the poet wrote:

> With the same soaring genius thy Lewis descends.
> And, seizing the car of the sun,
> O'er the sky-popping hills and high waters he bends
> And gives the proud earth a new zone
>
> Potowmack, Ohio, Missouri, has felt
> Half her globe in their cincture comprest;
> His long curving course has completed the belt,
> And tamed the last tide of the West.

Honors

President Jefferson appointed Lewis governor-general of the Louisiana Territory, with powers that stretched from St. Louis (the territorial capital) to the Rockies. William Clark was made a brigadier general of militia and Indian superintendent for the same area. The two captains seemed fated to continue in glorious tandem, as two of the most famous Americans of their time.

It was not to be, however.

Troubles

Lewis and Clark both moved to St. Louis in 1807. The captains followed separate paths for the next two years. The two men were not estranged, but the extreme closeness of their time on the expedition now was replaced by their attention to separate duties. Clark excelled in his position as Indian superintendent. He had shown himself to be a good diplomat during the expedition, and he now became the leading "Indian man" on the frontier. Lewis, on the other hand, was in a job that worked against his natural tendencies.

By nature, Lewis was a wanderer; he loved to move around. This man, who had walked 30 miles in a single day or paddled up to 80 miles in a canoe, was not at his best as a government official. He may have been cooped up in the days when he worked as President Jefferson's personal secretary, but that job had been different. Jefferson and Lewis were Virginians, and they understood each other very well. Both men thrived on freedom. In this new post as governor-general of Louisiana, Lewis was not a good keeper of records and accounts. To the historian and biographer, this indicates some change in his personality. Furthermore, Lewis's handwriting, which was seen so frequently in the expedition journals, had been neat, strong, and regular. Now, it was not. Something changed in 1807 and 1808, and Lewis's reputation suffered as a result.

Did Lewis's wound of 1806—the rifle ball in his backside—have anything to do with the change? It is not likely.

Had Lewis caught a disease on the expedition that weakened him? Possibly.

Did he suffer from a natural tendency toward melancholia, or what modern observers might call depression? Perhaps.

Whatever the cause, Lewis was heading toward an unhappy end.

Death

By the autumn of 1809, Lewis was in a bad way. His personal finances were in reasonably good condition, but his accounts for the management of the Louisiana Territory were not. He also had lost his patron in the White House. Thomas Jefferson had gone home to Monticello in March 1809. The new president was another Virginian, James Madison. Worst of all, perhaps, Lewis and Jefferson now were on cool terms. This was, in part, because Lewis had not yet arranged the papers and published the journals of the expedition. For these reasons and perhaps others, Lewis traveled eastward that September.

One of Lewis's last letters went to President Madison:

Dear Sir,

I arrived here [*at Chickasaw Bluffs, now Memphis, Tennessee*] yesterday, very much exhausted from the heat of the climate, but having taken medicine feel very much better this morning. . . . Provided my health permits no time shall be lost in reaching Washington. My anxiety to _____ [*space per Lewis's letter*] and to fulfill the duties incident to the internal arrangements incident to the government of Louisiana have prevented my writing you more frequently.

There is something strange about this letter. Complaints about heat and exhaustion had not previously been part of Meriwether Lewis's vocabulary. He formerly had shown resistance to such difficulties. The handwriting, too, shows changes from that of the expedition journals. The letter is filled with cross-outs, and the writing indicates a hasty pen. None of this is proof of anything, of course. It only suggests that Meriwether Lewis was under serious strain in the autumn of 1809.

Lewis arrived at Grinder's Inn, on the Natchez Trace trail in Tennessee, on the afternoon of October 11, 1809. To Priscilla Grinder, Lewis appeared tired, hungry, and unwell. Later, she gave several testimonies, all of which disagreed on some of the details. The essence of her story, however, is this: Her husband, the innkeeper, was away. Lewis retired for the evening, and she was awakened during the night by gunshots and screaming. She did not venture out until morning, when she found Meriwether Lewis in bed with a bullet wound in his chest. She claimed that his last words came in that early morning: "I am no coward but I am so strong. It is so hard to die."

The Verdict

The verdict on Lewis's death has never been reached. Scholars, historians, biographers, and psychologists still ask these questions:

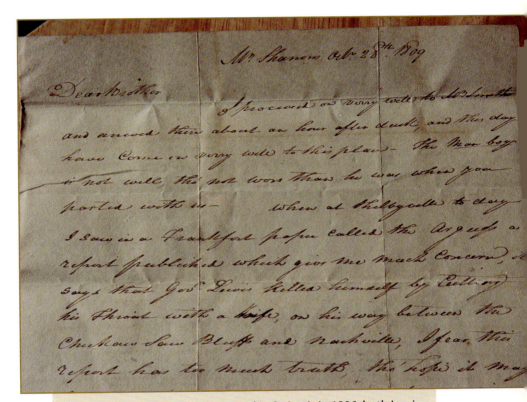

After the Corps of Discovery arrived in St. Louis in 1806, both Lewis and Clark were given political appointments as rewards for their hard work. Though Clark flourished in his position working with the Department of Indian Affairs, Lewis struggled to adjust to his new role as the governor-general of Louisiana Territory and was later found dead from a gunshot wound in 1809. Clark, in a letter to his brother *(above)*, fears Lewis has committed suicide.

Did Meriwether Lewis kill himself?

Was he murdered?

A large majority of people who have studied the matter—perhaps as many as 90 percent—believe that it was a case of suicide. They point to Lewis's low spirits and to the deterioration of his handwriting in the letter to President Madison. Some researchers believe that Lewis always had had a depressive temperament. (Historian Stephen Ambrose was among the leaders in this opinion.) Other experts think that the events of 1807–1809 brought him low. There are some people, however, who think that Lewis was murdered.

The Natchez Trace was a dangerous region. It was full of pickpockets, petty thieves, and the occasional murderer. It is possible that someone murdered Meriwether Lewis on the night of October 10, 1809, but a motive is lacking. Lewis's cash and valuables were not taken. Historian John D.W. Guice (one of the foremost of those who believe that Lewis might have been murdered) points out that the National Park Service has failed to be of help in this matter. Between 1996 and 2002, people petitioned the National Park Service three times to allow Lewis's body to be dug up and examined. All of the requests were denied.

Clark

William Clark lived for another 30 years. He died, famous and honored, in 1839. Clark had been the United States government's chief Indian agent for all of those years, and his fame had grown with the passage of time. Washington Irving, one of the first great American novelists, visited with Clark in 1832. Irving's notes suggest that the captain was as mentally sharp as ever.

The Two Captains

Lewis and Clark left plentiful journals that tell us a great deal about their discoveries but very little about themselves. Clark seems to have been almost entirely what his public presence suggested: a bold, skillful man who played a great part in a great enterprise. Lewis appears to have had more sides to his character. A reader of the journals senses a certain sensitivity and depth in this man who could write of buffalo, birds, American Indians, and war with the same easy grace. Yet it was Clark who lived on to tell the tale, and Lewis who died at the age of 35.

One thing is almost certain: The two captains liked, admired, and trusted each other. There is not the slightest indication, in the journals or elsewhere, that there was any conflict between them. In view of the fact that they were such different men, this was a notable achievement.

The Journals

At the time of Lewis's death, he had possession of the entire set of journals that he and Clark had written between 1804 and 1806. Thomas Jefferson sent for them and they were carried to Philadelphia, where they remained for the next few years. The U.S. government hired a young lawyer named Nicholas Biddle to edit the journals for publication. In 1814, at long last, the public had its first opportunity to purchase and read the journals of the Lewis and Clark Expedition.

Biddle did an excellent job as editor of the journals. He edited out much of the material about natural history, however. The reading public, therefore, saw Lewis and Clark as great pioneers but did not know that they also were pioneering naturalists. Not until 1904, when a new edition of the journals was published, did readers learn that Lewis and Clark had identified hundreds of varieties of animals and plants, and that they had been the first to identify the gray wolf and the snow goose, among other creatures. The editor of this new, more complete edition was Reuben Thwaites.

Other editions of the journals appeared during the twentieth century, most notably one edited by Bernard de Voto in 1953, and one by Gary Moulton in 1981. Then, toward the end of the century, historian Stephen Ambrose rekindled interest in the story of Lewis and Clark with a monumental book called *Undaunted Courage: Meriwether Lewis, Thomas Jefferson, and the Opening of the American West*. This book appeared in 1996, not long before the bicentennial of the expedition, and it made Lewis and Clark live again for thousands, if not millions, of readers.

HISTORY

OF

THE EXPEDITION

UNDER THE COMMAND OF

CAPTAINS LEWIS AND CLARK,

TO

THE SOURCES OF THE MISSOURI,

THENCE

ACROSS THE ROCKY MOUNTAINS

AND DOWN THE

RIVER COLUMBIA TO THE PACIFIC OCEAN.

PERFORMED DURING THE YEARS 1804—5—6.

By order of the

GOVERNMENT OF THE UNITED STATES.

PREPARED FOR THE PRESS

BY PAUL ALLEN, ESQUIRE.

IN TWO VOLUMES.

VOL. I.

PHILADELPHIA:

PUBLISHED BY BRADFORD AND INSKEEP; AND
ABM. H. INSKEEP, NEWYORK.

J. Maxwell, Printer.

1814.

Five years after Lewis's death, an official account of his and Clark's expedition was published in Philadelphia. Immensely popular with the public, the story of Lewis and Clark will forever be known as one of the greatest adventures in U.S. history.

The Nation

By 1839, the year Clark died, the red, white, and blue of the United States flag flew from Washington, D.C., to the Oregon Country. California was not yet a state, and the status of Texas still was in dispute with Mexico. Americans across the length and breadth of the country knew, however, that in the years from 1804 to 1806, two captains, their men, one woman, and a baby boy had done a great thing for the United States. They had extended the reach of the Stars and Stripes to the Pacific Northwest. There it remains.

CHRONOLOGY

1770	William Clark is born in Caroline County, Virginia.
1774	Meriwether Lewis is born in Albemarle County, Virginia.
1794	Ensign Lewis serves under Captain Clark.
1799	Napoleon Bonaparte becomes First Consul of France.
1800	Napoleon forces Spain to yield Louisiana to France.
1801	Thomas Jefferson is inaugurated as the third president of the United States.

TIMELINE

1803

Jefferson asks Congress to authorize exploratory expedition

1805

Lewis and Clark name the three branches of the Missouri River; Lewis crosses the Continental Divide

1806

AUGUST Reunion of Lewis and Clark; Lewis shot and wounded by Pierre Cruzatte

SEPTEMBER The corps returns to St. Louis, Missouri

1807

MARCH Corps enters the Rocky Mountains from the west; splits into two parties; plans to reunite at the Yellowstone-Missouri confluence. Lewis and party attacked by the Blackfeet

Lewis made governor of the Louisiana Territory

1803   Jefferson asks Congress to authorize an exploratory expedition into the American West.

James Monroe and Robert Livingston negotiate the Louisiana Purchase.

SEPTEMBER   Lewis leaves Pittsburgh.

1804   MAY   The Corps of Discovery leaves Wood Camp; Sergeant Charles Floyd dies.

SEPTEMBER   The Corps of Discovery meets the Teton Sioux.

NOVEMBER   The Corps of Discovery reaches the Mandan villages.

1805   MARCH   The corps leaves the Mandan villages.

MAY   The corps reaches the confluence of the Yellowstone and Missouri rivers.

JUNE   The corps reaches the Marias River.

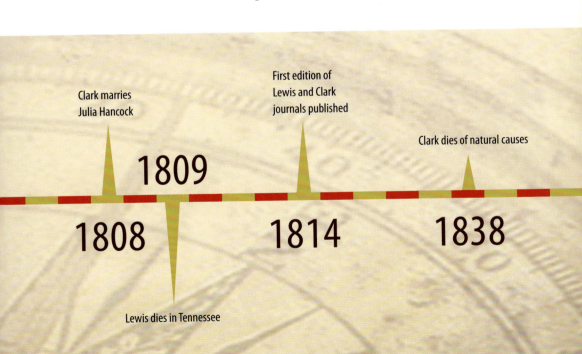

Clark marries Julia Hancock

First edition of Lewis and Clark journals published

Clark dies of natural causes

1809

1808   **1814**   **1838**

Lewis dies in Tennessee

Lewis and Clark reach the Great Falls of the Missouri.

JULY   Lewis and Clark name the three branches of the Missouri River.

AUGUST   Lewis crosses the Continental Divide.

Lewis meets Cameahwait.

SEPTEMBER   Lewis, Clark, and the corps are guided by Old Toby.

OCTOBER   The corps reaches the Snake River.

The corps reaches the Columbia River.

NOVEMBER   The corps enters the estuary of the Columbia River.

DECEMBER   The corps settles into Fort Clatsop.

1806   JANUARY   The corps journeys to see a dead whale.

MARCH   The corps leaves Fort Clatsop and enters the Rocky Mountains from the west; the corps splits into two parties; the parties plan to reunite at the Yellowstone-Missouri confluence.

Lewis and his party are attacked by the Blackfeet.

AUGUST   Reunion of Lewis and Clark.

Lewis is shot and wounded by Pierre Cruzatte.

SEPTEMBER   The corps returns to St. Louis, Missouri.

1807   Lewis is made governor of the Louisiana Territory.

1808   Clark marries Julia Hancock.

1809   Lewis dies in Tennessee.

1814   The first edition of Lewis and Clark's journals is published.

1838   Clark dies of natural causes.

1870   Patrick Gass, the oldest living member of the corps, dies at age 99.

GLOSSARY

BLACKFEET An American Indian tribe that lived on the northern Great Plains.

CONFLUENCE The joining of two rivers. One example is the joining of the Missouri and the Mississippi rivers, just above St. Louis, Missouri.

CORPS OF DISCOVERY Technical name for the men (and one woman) who went westward with Lewis and Clark.

CREOLE A term that describes the mixture of two cultures; it often is used to describe a mixture of Spanish and French.

IMPRESSMENT A policy of the British government by which British naval vessels seized American sailors from their ships and pressed them into service in the Royal Navy.

KEELBOAT A type of boat used as one of the most common ways to travel on the Ohio, Missouri, and Mississippi rivers.

MANDAN An American Indian tribe that lived in what is now South Dakota.

PIROGUE A type of keelboat used on the Lewis and Clark expedition.

BIBLIOGRAPHY

Ambrose, Stephen. *Undaunted Courage: Meriwether Lewis, Thomas Jefferson, and the Opening of the American West.* New York: Simon & Schuster, 1996.

Betts, Robert. *In Search of York: The Slave Who Went to the Pacific with Lewis and Clark.* Boulder: University Press of Colorado, 2002.

Clarke, Charles G. *Men of the Lewis and Clark Expedition.* Lincoln: University of Nebraska Press, 2002.

DeVoto, Bernard, ed. *The Journals of Lewis and Clark.* Boston: Houghton Mifflin, 1954.

Dillon, Richard. *Meriwether Lewis: A Biography.* New York: Coward McCann, 1965.

Guice, John D.W., ed. *By His Own Hand? The Mysterious Death of Meriwether Lewis.* Norman: University of Oklahoma Press, 2006.

"Inside the Corps," PBS.com. Available online at http://www.pbs.org/lewisandclark/inside/index.html.

"Lewis and Clark: The Journey of the Corps of Discovery," PBS Home Video, (DVD), 1997.

Josephy, Alvin, ed. *Lewis and Clark Through Indian Eyes: Nine Indian Writers on the Legacy of the Expedition.* New York: Random House, 2006.

The Journals of Lewis and Clark, abridged by Anthony Brandt and with an afterword by Herman J. Viola. Washington, D.C.: National Geographic Adventure Classics, 2003.

Lewis, Meriwether. *The Original Journals of the Lewis and Clark Expedition, 1804–1806,* edited by Reuben Gold Thwaites. New York: Dodd, Mead & Company, 1905.

Our Documents: 100 Milestone Documents from the National Archives. New York: Oxford University Press, 2003.

FURTHER RESOURCES

Danisi, Thomas C., and John C. Jackson. *Meriwether Lewis*. Amherst, N.Y.: Prometheus Books, 2009.

Dillon, Richard. *Meriwether Lewis: A Biography*. Lafayette, Calif.: Great West Books, 2003.

Foley, William E. *Wilderness Journey: The Life of William Clark*. Columbia: University of Missouri Press, 2006.

Gragg, Rod. *Lewis and Clark on the Trail of Discovery: An Interactive History with Removable Artifacts*. Nashville, Tenn.: Thomas Nelson, 2003.

Jones, Landon Y. *The Essential Lewis and Clark*. New York: Harper-Perennial, 2002.

Josephy, Alvin M. Jr., ed. *Lewis and Clark Through Indian Eyes: Nine Indian Writers on the Legacy of the Expedition*. New York: Vintage, 2007.

Schanzer, Rosalyn. *How We Crossed the West: The Adventures of Lewis and Clark*. Washington, D.C.: National Geographic Children's Books, 2002.

Summitt, April R. *Sacagawea: A Biography*. Santa Barbara, Calif.: Greenwood Press, 2008.

FILM AND RECORDINGS

Lewis and Clark: Great Journey West—National Geographic (DVD), 2002

Lewis and Clark: The Journey of the Corps of Discovery (Soundtrack), 2003

Sacagawea: Heroine of the Lewis and Clark Journey (DVD), 2004

WEB SITES

Journals of the Lewis and Clark Expedition

http://lewisandclarkjournals.unl.edu/

This site features the full text—almost 5,000 pages—of the journals. It also includes a gallery of images, supplemental text, and audio files from the American Indians' perspectives.

Lewis and Clark

http://www.nps.gov/lecl/

Over 200 years after the Lewis and Clark expedition traveled from Illinois to the Pacific Ocean, visitors can retrace their path. Information is provided by the U.S. Department of the Interior National Park Service site about how to plan a visit to the Lewis and Clark National Historical Trail.

Lewis and Clark Fort Mandan Foundation of Washburn, North Dakota (formerly Discovering Lewis & Clark)

http://www.lewis-clark.org/content/content-channel.asp?ChannelID=256

A comprehensive site about the Lewis and Clark expedition. It features a synopsis about the expedition, graphics, color images, and journal excerpts.

Lewis and Clark: Mapping the West

http://www.edgate.com/lewisandclark/

This site, sponsored by the Smithsonian National Museum of Natural History, provides detailed information about the expedition, the tribes and cultures Lewis and Clark came into contact with, and the routes that were taken. Features black-and-white and color images, learning activities, and lesson plans for educators and students.

National Geographic Lewis & Clark Interactive Journey Log

http://www.nationalgeographic.com/lewisandclark/

Offers customized journey log, photographs, maps, and interactive activities to interest and entertain young readers.

PICTURE CREDITS

INDEX

ABOUT THE AUTHOR

SAMUEL WILLARD CROMPTON lives near the Westfield River, which cuts through the Berkshire Hills of his native western Massachusetts—a far cry from the Rocky Mountains or the Missouri. His interest in the American West began in his twenties, and he has contributed sections on explorers and exploration to a number of works, including the *American National Biography* and the *Illustrated Atlas of Native American History*. He teaches history at Westfield State College and Holyoke Community College.